Old Organs of Princeton

The 1875 Geo. Jardine & Son organ in the First Presbyterian Church (over).

Old Organs of Princeton

*Being an Historical Chronology and
Description of all the known Pipe Organs
installed in the
Town of Princeton, New Jersey,
from 1760 to 1925,
including Photographs and Stoplists when available,
as well as Accounts from Newspapers,
Church Records, Histories, and Diaries*

By Stephen L. Pinel

The Boston Organ Club Chapter of
The Organ Historical Society
Harrisville, New Hampshire
1989

© 1989 by The Boston Organ Club

Library of Congress Cataloging in Publication Data:
        Pinel, Stephen Leigh, 1956–
        Old Organs of Princeton . . .
        Library of Congress Card Number: 89-62170
        ML 561
        .P653

        ISBN 0-9610092-25

★ ★ ★ ★ ★

Copy number _____ of 700

_____

To Eugene Roan

No student ever had a better teacher.

Art acknowledges no authority in custom or in the prerogatives of Science until Taste sanctions the decrees. The criteria of Taste simply reflect the data of individual education or experience. The Soul of Art is born of universal and eternal principles; but local and temporary influences mold and modify her protean features. Musicians, therefore, with poets and artists, are creatures of their day and place.

From a circa 1905 Hillgreen, Lane & Co. Catalogue.

Table of Contents.

List of Photographs and Sources.
All photographs used with permission

Frontispiece:
1. The First Church, interior, glass plate c. 1890, showing the 1875 George Jardine & Son organ located at the front of the sanctuary. Source: Princeton Historical Society.

Chapter I:
2. Samuel Davies (1723-61), fourth President of the College of New Jersey. Source: Princeton University Archives.
3. Ezra Stiles (1727-95). Source: Princeton University Archives.
4. An 1844 woodcut of the College of New Jersey showing Nassau Hall. Source: Princeton University Archives.
5. The Old College Chapel, built in 1847, exterior. Source: Princeton University Archives.
6. Benjamin Morehouse. Source: Princeton University Archives.
7. Samuel Pennington (1806-1900). Source: Princeton University Archives.
8. The Old College Chapel, interior, stereopticon slide, circa 1870, showing the 1860 organ built by Ernest Hartwick. Source: Princeton University Archives.
9. Thomas S. Hall (1794-1874). Source: The American Organ Archive.
10. First Presbyterian Church, exterior, 1872. Source: First Church Archives, Princeton Theological Seminary.
11. George Jardine (1800-82). Source: The American Organ Archive.
12. George W. Morgan (1822-92). Source: *The Organ*, edited by Everette Truette.
13. Arthur D. Walbridge (d. 1872), choir director at the First Presbyterian Church during 1863. Source: Princeton University Archives.
14. Second Presbyterian Church, interior, 1912, showing an organ built by an unidentified maker in the rear gallery. Source: *The Princeton Packet*, Wednesday, 17 February 1965.

Chapter II:
15. Karl Langlotz (1834-1915). Source: Princeton University Archives.

Chapter III:
16. First Church, interior, woodcut of 1875 George Jardine & Son organ at the front of the building. Source: "Commencement Day," *Leslie's Weekly*, 6 July 1878.

17. John C. Pennington (1850-97). Source: Princeton University Archives.
18. Program of Exhibition, 17 January 1871. Source: Princeton University Archives.
19. William Augustus Muhlenberg Diller (1836-71). Source: A. H. Messiter, *A History of the Choir and Music of Trinity Church, New York From Its Organization, to the Year 1897.* (New York: Edwin S. Gorham, 1906), p. 112a.
20. Old College Chapel, interior, c. 1880, showing Hall & Labagh organ. Source: Princeton University Archives.
21. Old College Chapel, interior, c. 1880, detail. Source: Princeton University Archives.
22. Marquand Chapel, exterior, c. 1900. Source: Princeton University Archives.
23. Marquand Chapel, interior, c. 1890. Source: Princeton University Archives.
24. Marquand Chapel, interior, c. 1900, showing Müller & Abel organ. Source: Princeton University Archives.
25. Müller & Abel advertisement. Source: The American Organ Archive.
26. Henry Clay Briggs (1872-1964). Source: Princeton University Archives.
27. George Jardine & Son organ factory taken from their 1890 catalogue. Source: The American Organ Archive.
28. The employees of George Jardine & Son, New York, c. 1895. Source: The American Organ Archive.
29. Alexander Hall, Princeton University, 1986, showing the facade of the George Jardine & Son organ. Photo credit: author.
30. Alexander Hall, interior, detail, 1986. Photo credit: author.
31. J.H. & C.S. Odell advertisement from *The American Musical Directory*, 1861. (New York: Thomas Hutchinson, 1861), p. 263.
32. Henry Stephen Culter (1824-1902). Source: A. H. Messiter, *A History of the Choir and Music of Trinity Church, New York From Its Organization, to the Year 1897.* (New York: Edwin S. Gorham, 1906). p. 72a.
33. Trinity Church, interior, glass plate, c. 1890, showing keydesk of J.H. & C.S. Odell, Opus 111 (1872). Source: Princeton Historical Society.
34. Trinity Church, interior, glass plate, c. 1890, showing facade of J.H. & C.S. Odell, Opus 111 (1872). Source: Princeton Historical Society.

Chapter IV:

Foreword.

This elegant volume is indeed a milestone in American organ research. There are numerous European books dealing with the instruments in a particular locality, but organ enthusiasts in the Western Hemisphere have never enjoyed or produced such a publication. Articles in periodicals, often quite scantily researched, have discussed a considerable array of builders and communities that were and are part of the three centuries that pipe organs have been heard in North America.

Mr. Pinel is to be commended for his pioneering and enlightening survey of the earlier organs in one well-known Eastern town, a representative array of instruments from Colonial times to the present. Princeton was and is a cultured atmosphere, even though it never savored the refined sounds of a Hook or Johnson installation. Its citizens turned almost exclusively to New York builders for larger organs until the advent of the famous four-manual 1927 E.M. Skinner placed in the University Chapel.

Unfortunately, we are living in an age of suppositious research and "facts" are contrived by historians who do little basic looking into such obvious sources as church records and newspapers. In word-processor haste, books, articles, and recording jacket notes are rushed into print without adequate footnotes, without a single fellow historian allowed to read the manuscript, without checking of proof pages before the presses run, and without thought of ever issuing corrections and additions. Examples of such faulty writing are too well-known to mention here.

So, here we have a book prepared with enthusiasm, good humor, great care, and patience during several years. Many of the author's friends and mentors have given assistance to perfect a work that was excellent in its first draft. Every available or willing source has been checked, and unlike writers who refuse to leave any mysteries for future organologists to solve, Mr. Pinel is willing to admit what is not yet known. He is a researcher and musician of the first rank, whose articles published here and abroad show him to be a conscientious historian. Few works on so esoteric a subject as the long-gone organs in one town are "sold out" before they are printed.

Nearly every major community deserves a study of both its vanished and tangible organs. Regrettably, few are the authors who have the time to do what has been done for Princeton. May *Old Organs of Princeton*, and its apparent success, encourage other writers to follow in Mr. Pinel's worthy footsteps.

E. A. Boadway
Editor of Publications
The Boston Organ Club

Introduction.

Organs come in an astonishing variety of shapes and sizes, and the singularity of each individual instrument is far more apparent than it is with other musical instruments. Organs can be large or small, voiced gently or loudly, intimate or majestic, mechanical or electric, plain or decorated, and so on. Throughout the centuries, the organ has been a source of inspiration, not only to exalted minds like those of Johann Sebastian Bach and Albert Schweitzer, but to the members of the local church. Honoré de Balzac put it succinctly when he wrote, "The Organ is surely some sort of pedestal on which the soul poises for a flight into space . . ."

For more than two centuries, Princeton organs have played a significant role in the cultural fabric and development of the community. They have adorned places of public worship, not only with ecclesiastical music, but visually with their cases; they have accompanied baptisms, confirmations, graduations, marriages, and funerals; they have been used at concerts. Moreover, how many times have we sung accompanied by an organ without being cognizant of the crucial function the instrument plays in our faith?

Princeton, with its history of affluence, has enjoyed a long tradition of fascinating organs: from the unidentified instrument of about 1760, placed in Nassau Hall, to the controversial George Jardine & Son organ built for Mexico but installed in the First Presbyterian Church during 1864; from the large Aeolian & Co. organ in Procter Hall, donated by Henry Clay Frick in 1916, to the monumental Ernest M. Skinner organ in the University Chapel. Many engaging stories are hidden in church records, diaries, newspapers, and music journals, which are now collected for the first time.

Numerous individuals assisted in the compilation of this history. Foremost was the invaluable support of Earle Coleman, University Archivist, who graciously unlocked the riches of Princeton University Archives. Their collection of newspapers, record books, and memorabilia is superbly organized and carefully maintained, and many of the photographs published in this book originated there. Other materials housed at the Princeton Historical Society and the Princeton Public Library answered many questions; the staff at those institutions, often volunteers, were always ready to be of assistance. The individual churches, especially Nassau Presbyterian Church and Trinity Episcopal Church, also deserve mention for allowing access to minute books, photographs, and other historical documents.

The American Organ Archive of The Organ Historical Society provided stoplists, photographs, some company records, and the source material on each of the individual firms. Frederick Mitchell, of the Austin Organ Co., Inc., and Ronald R. Ellis, of M.P. Möller, Inc., deserve sincere thanks for providing historical material from company files.

Heartfelt thanks is extended to E. A. Boadway, Earle Coleman, Alan M. Laufman, and my mother and father for their conscientious proof-reading, and to the Boston Organ Club, for sponsoring this publication. Thomas McBeth set the type and designed the page layout, and offered many suggestions, all of which made this a finer piece of scholarship.

Stephen L. Pinel
Princeton, New Jersey
September, 1989

Chapter I:
The First Organs in Town.

Princeton, New Jersey, has always held a pre-eminent place in the annals of American history. The village hosted a meeting of the Continental Congress, it boasted an important victory during the Revolution, and — unknown to most Americans — it was the capital of the United States during 1783. It was in the capital building, Nassau Hall (owned by the College of New Jersey), that the first use of an organ in the town of Princeton is recorded.

The origin of that instrument is a mystery, but like many eighteenth century American organs, it may have been imported. A published account of the College of New Jersey, dated 1764, states:

> [Nassau Hall has a room] of genteel workmanship,
> being a square of near 40 feet, with a neatly finished front
> gallery. Here is a small, tho' exceeding good organ,
> which was obtained by a voluntary subscription: Oppo-
> site to which, and of the same height, is erected a stage,
> for the use of the students, in their public exhibitions.[1]

Reputedly, the organ was installed during or about 1760, when authorization was given to substitute psalms for scripture readings at vespers.[2]

Collins, author of the monograph, *Princeton*, attributes the innovation to Samuel Davies (1723-61),[3] then president of the college,

---

1. *An Account of the College of New Jersey: In which are Described the Methods of Government, Modes of Instruction, Manner of Expenses of Living in the same, &c.* (Wood-bridge, New Jersey: James Parker, 1764), p. 12.

2. Varnum Lansing Collins, *Princeton.* (New York: Oxford University Press, 1914), p. 56.

3. It is not surprising that Samuel Davies may have been responsible for both an

I

Samuel Davies, President of the College of New Jersey.

and James Lyon (1735-94),[4] one of America's first native musicians, who graduated from the institution in 1759, and received his M.A. degree in 1762.[5] Lyon held a prominent place in the collegiate musical community: at his own undergraduate commencement on 26 September 1759, he wrote the music for an entertainment ode, prob-

organ and liturgical innovations at the College of New Jersey considering his reputation. For additional information see George William Pilcher, *Samuel Davies, Apostle of Dissent in Colonial Virginia.* (Knoxville, [Tennessee]: The University of Tennessee Press, [1971]).

4. *Op. cit.*, no. 2.

5. *The New Grove Dictionary of American Music*, "James Lyon," by Richard Crawford. ([London: MacMillan Limited, and New York: Grove's Dictionaries of Music, Inc., 1986]).

ably to a text by Davies.[6] Two years later, Lyon issued *Urania* (1761), said to comprise the first newly composed (or arranged) music used in the college chapel.[7] Then in 1763, Lyon probably wrote the music for another ode, *A Dialogue of Peace, an Entertainment, Given by the Senior Class at the Anniversary Commencement, Held at Nassau Hall . . .*[8] Despite Collins' presumed correlation between Lyon and the organ, there appears to be no connection other than the fact that Lyon was a Princetonian at the time the organ was acquired.

Nor is it apparent exactly how the organ was used. Thomas Jefferson Wertenbaker, author of *Princeton: 1746-1896*, asserts, "after the erection of Nassau Hall [in 1756] the trustees gave . . . evidence of their approval of music as a part of religious exercises by placing an organ in Prayer Hall."[9] This and similar statements in other sources hearken to the diary of Ezra Stiles (1727-95),[10] who in 1770 wrote that the organ was "an innovation of ill consequence," of which they soon became a "little sick."[11] Stiles never precisely clarifies how the organ was used, leaving that point to conjecture.[12] However, one fact is certain: Prayer Hall, as the 1764 account describes, was a multi-purpose gathering space not intended solely for ecclesiastical functions, and it is possible that the organ was used for non-religious purposes.

One likelihood was commencement. The musical portions of

6. Earle E. Coleman, "New & Notable: *A Dialogue on Peace* (1763) and Princeton Commencements." *The Princeton University Chronicle*, v. 46, no. 2 (Winter, 1985), p. 232-233; and O. G. Sonneck, *Francis Hopkinson and James Lyon: Two Studies in American Music.* (Washington D.C.: H. L. McQueen, 1905), p. 121-133.

7. *Ibid.*

8. *Ibid.*

9. Thomas Jefferson Wertenbaker, *Princeton: 1746-1896.* (Princeton, New Jersey: Princeton University Press, 1946), p. 197-198.

10. Ezra Stiles entered Yale in 1743 and graduated in 1746. In 1753 he took up law and became an attorney, and he later received the D.D. degree from Dartmouth and Princeton. It was during these years that Stiles came in contact with the small circa 1760 organ in the College Chapel, and wrote about it in his diary. Stiles also commented on other eighteenth century American organs including the 1727 organ at the South Dutch Reformed Church in New York City. See John Ogasapian, *Organ Building in New York City: 1700-1900.* (Braintree, Massachusetts: The Organ Literature Foundation, 1977), p. 2.

11. *The Literary Diary of Ezra Stiles,* I, p. 58, as cited in Thomas Jefferson Wertenbaker, *Princeton: 1746-1896.* (Princeton, New Jersey: Princeton University Press, 1946), p. 197-198.

12. *The Literary Diary of Ezra Stiles, D.D., LL.D. President of Yale College.* Edited

the 1763 graduation ode (thought to be composed by Lyon) have survived; they consist of solo songs with a two-part treble and bass accompaniment. Whereas the score fails to designate any specific instrument(s), the part could have been played on the organ.

Other possible uses for the instrument might have included plays and dramatic presentations, or in connection with the student orchestra, which Stiles also recalled in his diary. However it was used, the organ came to an unfortunate end: its pipes fell prey to Revolutionary War soldiers who used the metal to make bullets.[13]

Three quarters of a century passed before there was mention of another organ at the College. Describing the events of 1848, a writer later noted:

> Suspicion and dissatisfaction increased when the students of their own volition, started a subscription for an organ in the chapel. Organ music might be appropriate for an Episcopal church, but it was out of place with . . . Presbyterian congregational singing. "I do not know that the Faculty have sanctioned it," Isaac V. Brown wrote to Samuel Miller, "but I do think they ought to arrest the measure instantly . . ."[14]

Another letter, from Cortlandt Van Rensselaer (1808-60) to Dr. John Maclean (1800-86), president of the institution from 1854-68, concurs with the account by Brown:

> Sometime in 1848, after the students had been a short time in the new Chapel . . . the young gentlemen took it into their hands to have an organ . . .
>
> I am satisfied that a majority of the Trustees are opposed to an organ . . . But after the organ gets up . . . the trustees will sit in their new arm chairs and quietly say . . . "It's too late."[15]

---

by Franklin Bowditch Dexter, v. 1. (New York: Charles Scribner's Sons, 1901), p. 58.

13. *Op. cit.*, no. 9.
14. *Ibid.*, p. 241.
15. MS, Letter, Cortlandt Van Rensselaer to Rev. Dr. Maclean, 14 March 1848.

Ezra Stiles, Pastor.

The builder of this instrument is not known, and the Chapel at the College of New Jersey is not found on any known organbuilder's list or promotional material of the era. The building was erected in 1847 to a design by architect John Notman (1810-65), of Philadelphia.[16] We might hazard a guess then, that the instrument could

16. Notman also furnished the design for the first building of the Second Presbyterian Church of Princeton, in 1850. See Constance M. Greiff, *John Notman, Architect, 1810-1865.* ([Philadelphia]: The Athenaeum of Philadelphia, 1979), p. 149-150.

The College of New Jersey in 1844.

have been made by a Philadelphia maker, perhaps John C. B. Standbridge (1800-71), Henry Knauff, or even Henry Corrie (1786-1859), because the architect was a Philadelphian.

A new instrument was installed during November, 1860, primarily through the efforts of Benjamin Morehouse, director of the college choir. Morehouse wrote:

Nov. 6th, 1860

[Dr. Maclean:]

I must ask your pardon for not informing you sooner of my doings. I set my mind upon getting an *Organ*, and although delayed by stormy weather for a few days, I have presented the matter to several Trustees in the city, and it meets their hearty approval. Dr. [Samuel] Pennington [1806-1900] is particularly anxious; he is an excellent judge in such matters, and I have deferred to his judgement, so as to do nothing rashly. He has examined an instrument now building and is entirely satisfied with it, and says that it is very desirable that we should secure it. I set to work calling upon the friends of the College in the city, and, had it not been for the political excitement, I should have secured funds nearly sufficient to have paid entirely for the instrument. The maker is desirous to put it up for us, and will do so very reasonably, and give me time to make my collections. Thus, we shall have a *very fine* organ. Giving our old instrument in we get it for $650 net. It is worth $900... I suspect it will arrive by Saturday, or first of next week . . .

I am your humble servant,
B. S. Morehouse[17]

Three weeks later, an anonymous reporter in the local newspaper noted:

For the Princeton Press.
NEW ORGAN FOR THE COLLEGE CHAPEL.
– All visitors to the College Chapel must have noticed the old organ, which has stood in the gallery for the last fifteen years. But last week this old organ was removed, and a splendid new instrument substituted, made by Mr. Ernest Hartwick, a builder of considerable experience, of Newark in our State, at a cost of about $1000. The funds have been nearly secured, being subscribed by friends and graduates, together with contributions from

The Old College Chapel, built in 1847.

17. MS, Letter, Benjamin Morehouse to Rev. Dr. Maclean, 6 November 1860.

Benjamin Morehouse, director of the choir at the College of New Jersey.

the students themselves. This new organ was exhibited for the first time last Friday evening, and its excellence received the applause of the entire College . . .[18]

Hartwick initially appeared in the Newark City directory during 1855 as "Hartwick Ernest, organbuilder 18 Mill [street]."[19] He is listed until 1877, and then from 1880 until 1892, he is found as an "organtuner," residing much of the time at 19 Clay Street. Nothing has been written about Hartwick, and this instrument, built for Princeton College Chapel, is the only instrument definitely attributable to his shop.

Raising money by subscription was not as effortless as Morehouse anticipated. In a letter addressed to the Trustees of the

---

18. "New Organ for the College Chapel," *The Princeton Press*, 30 November 1860, p. 2.

19. B. T. Pierson, *Directory of the City of Newark, For 1855-56*. (Newark, N.J.: A. Stephen Holbrook, 1855). Hartwick is also listed in Thomas Hutchinson, *The American Musical Directory*. (New York: Thomas Huchinson, 1861), p. 84, at "Newark / 121 Market st."

Samuel Pennington.

College on 18 December 1860, Morehouse requested an appropriation of $400. He needed $200 to cover a subscription shortfall, and the remainder was a loan to pay Hartwick for the organ until the students returned at the beginning of the next session.

A full year later, the matter was still unsettled. An unhappy Hartwick wrote directly to Dr. Maclean:

> Newark, December 10th 1861
>
> Sir. Enclosed you will [find] the bill for the Organ built by me for the Princeton College Chappell [*sic*]. I hope you will present the bill to the board of Trustees at their next meeting to act upon. I must have the account settled by their next meeting. I sold the Organ to the Chappell for $100.00 less as I was promised cash in three months, but you will see by the bill how the account stands. If you think it will be necessary for me to be present at the Trustee Meeting, inform me what day

The interior of the Old College Chapel, showing the 1860 organ built by Ernest Hartwick.

they will meet and I will come down. I was at Princeton some three weeks ago to tune the Organ, and was very much disappointed at not being able to see you. Please inform me when the trustees meet . . .

    Yours truly,

               Ernest Hartwick[20]

The debt persisted. In a letter of 1863 to Dr. Maclean, Henry L.

---

20. MS, Letter, Ernest Hartwick to Rev. Dr. John Maclean, 10 December 1861.

Sampson noted:

> [I know] nothing whatever . . . in reference to the
> sums collected by Mr. Morehouse in order to pay for the
> organ . . . What led me to address you in the first place
> was partly consequent upon the surprise occasioned on
> hearing that the organ debt had not been cleared off long
> ago . . . Mr. Morehouse has been imposed upon by
> Hartwick – at least I should so judge from what I have
> heard from two of my classmates . . . I am glad that the
> prospect of getting the organ matter out of the way en-
> tirely is bright. Mr. Morehouse deserves commendation
> for his thoroughness . . .[21]

There is no further evidence to suggest that the debt lingered,
and presumably the builder received his money.

Some questioned the quality of the organ. Sampson continued:

> As I remember the old organ, it was a better instru-
> ment even under the weight of years than the new one in
> its new fledged dignity. I regret deeply that Morehouse
> put himself or the College under any sort of obligation to
> Hartwick if indeed he did. And I should judge that even
> under the present status, Hartwick had better restore the
> old organ and take the new, restoring also all payments
> made by Mr. Morehouse on behalf of the College except-
> ing so much as his trouble shall be deemed worth . . .[22]

The Hartwick organ remained in the chapel for only ten years,
and ultimately, this may be an indication of its quality. The Archives
of Princeton University preserve a stereoscopic image of this instrument: a three-sectional case shows a disproportionately large central
flat flanked by two smaller ones in a design not common for the
period. The organ was small, and appears to have had only one
manual. Between July and October, 1870, the building was en-

---

21. MS, Letter, Henry L. Sampson to Rev. Dr. Maclean, 29 April 1863.
22. *Ibid.*

larged, and a new instrument was ordered from Hall & Labagh, of New York. According to financial records of the college, the 1860 organ was sold on 25 August 1870 for $225. Though the ledger does not identify the buyer,[23] other sources confirm that St. Paul's Roman Catholic Church of Princeton was the purchaser, and this will be discussed later.

Meanwhile, several of the local church organizations acquired instruments of their own. Trinity Episcopal Church was organized in 1829, and the cornerstone for a small building was set on 4 July 1833.[24] There is no doubt that the parish had an organ from the beginning:

> On the day of consecration [23 September 1834] the organ was played by a [Princeton Theological] seminary student, Thomas Clark, who later became the presiding Bishop of the Church. He wrote, "No one being found to play the organ at the consecration, I volunteered my services. All that I have to say about it is that I was never asked to repeat the operation."[25]

No details of this instrument are known to exist, but it has the probable distinction of being the first organ used in any Princeton church. Later, "In 1842, . . . an organist named George Young succeeded a Mr. Smith. For the next twenty years the organ bench was occupied by a variety of volunteers, mostly women; the most distinguished of these volunteers was Prof. Karl Langlotz."[26]

Trinity Church acquired a new organ in 1850 from Hall & Labagh, and the stoplist of that instrument is preserved among the firm's correspondence.[27] The elder member of the partnership, Thomas S. Hall (1794-1874), was among the more prominent organ builders of his generation. In fact, Hall trained either directly or

---

23. MS, Financial Ledger, Princeton University, showing account for old organ.
24. Margery P. Cuyler and Nathanial Burt, *The History of Trinity Church, Princeton, New Jersey: 1833-1914.* (Published by the Church).
25. *Ibid.*
26. *Ibid.*
27. MS, Hall & Labagh Correspondence, v. II, p. 13.

Thomas S. Hall, organbuilder.

indirectly most of the nineteenth century organbuilders in New York, with the exception of George Jardine (1800-82). These men included Henry Erben (1800-84), Richard M. Ferris (1818-58), and Hall's partner in the firm, John Labagh (1810-91). The Hall & Labagh firm was founded in October, 1846, and continued to manufacture organs until 1891, when the company was sold.

Although the building of Trinity Church housed the first organ, it was not the oldest congregation in town. The First Presbyterian Church was established in 1755, when a group of local faithful petitioned the Presbytery at Lawrenceville to organize and build a meeting house.[28] The congregation was conservative, and although the idea of buying an organ was frequently discussed at parish meetings, it was not until 1863 that permission to acquire one was finally granted.[29] John F. Hageman, in his history of the Town of Princeton, noted:

> The introduction of an organ into the [first] church had frequently been suggested, but several families of rigid Presbyterian principles . . . who were slow to yield to any form of innovation upon the simple severities of the old school, had always expressed so much opposition to it that no decided action had ever been taken to secure one. But the number of such gradually grew less and less, principally by death. The subject encountered a discussion at a congregational meeting in 1863, which was followed by a resolution offered by Professor Cameron, "that it is expedient that instrumental music be employed in this church." This was adopted by a vote of 13 to 6. A committee was appointed to raise the funds. On the 4th of January, 1864, the congregation again met and directed the purchase of an organ . . .[30]

First mention of the organ in the Session Minutes of the congregation occurred during July of 1863, when:

---

28. Arthur S. Link, *The First Presbyterian Church of Princeton: Two Centuries of History.* (Princeton, New Jersey: The First Presbyterian Church, 1967), p. 9.

29. The First Church of Princeton was among the last area Presbyterian churches to acquire an organ. To the south, First Presbyterian Church in Trenton acquired an organ built by Holbrook & Ware in 1840. To the north, First Presbyterian Church, New Brunswick, bought a two-manual organ made by Hall & Labagh in 1851. First Presbyterian Church in Rahway, just north of New Brunswick, acquired an organ from Holbrook & Ware in 1836, and First Presbyterian Church, Elizabeth, had an 1840 instrument built by Henry Erben.

30. John Frelinghuysen Hageman, *History of Princeton and its Institutions . . .* (Philadelphia: J. B. Lippincott & Co., 1879), p. 157-158.

The First Presbyterian Church in 1872.

On motion, Resolved that Five dollars be appropriated from the contingent fund of the Session, to pay the expenses of Mr. Carl Langlotz, Musical Teacher, on his journey to New York & his return – Mr. Langlotz having agreed that he would make inquiries with respect to an organ or other musical instrument suitable for this church, and examine, and make report with respect to the same.[31]

On 4 March 1864, the local newspaper announced:

NEW ORGAN. – The Carpenters are at work on the gallery of the First Church, altering and preparing it for the reception of a large Organ, which will be erected and ready for use about the middle of this month.[32]

A week later, George W. Morgan's (1822-92) name was mentioned nine times in the local news column.[33] Noted as a concert organist, Morgan was frequently associated with the exhibition of

---

31. MS, Session Minutes, First Presbyterian Church, Princeton, New Jersey, Friday, 24 July 1863. Examined and quoted with permission of the church.
32. "New Organ," *Princeton Standard*, Friday, 4 March 1864, p. 3.
33. *Ibid.*, Friday, 11 March 1864, p. 3.

George W. Morgan, organist.

new instruments. Then follows an unfortunate gap in the Princeton newspapers, and the subsequent issue is missing.[34] Obviously, Morgan played a public concert, but it has been impossible to ascertain the date.

A follow-up notice occurred on April 15th:

THE NEW ORGAN. A new organ, built by Jardine & Son, of New York, to meet the order of a church in Mexico, but not sent there on account of obstructed transportation, has been procured and introduced into the First Presbyterian Church, of this place, its original price was $1800, but it was obtained for about $1600. It is adjudged to be an excellent instrument. — Encased in oiled chestnut, in a style not painfully remote from the Grecian architecture of the church, its appearance on the gallery is rather ornamental than otherwise. It is much larger than any other organ in town. It was stated by the pastor, that the money was raised by donations from about thirty persons in the congregation, and by the proceeds of a Fair and Lectures. Mr. [Arthur D.] Walbridge [d. 1872] of the College, who has led the choir during the last year, has taken a leading part in raising the Organ Fund, and perhaps to his perseverance in the cause the success of the movement is principally due . . .[35]

The article discussed the problems encountered in introducing instrumental music to a congregation not accustomed to it, and in conclusion noted:

It is probable that after the people shall become used to it, they will regard it as an indispensable aid to public worship. But whatever its future influence may be, its present effect is happy in increasing the attendance upon the ordinary services, especially the evening service, which during the last six months it is alleged have become strikingly diminished.[36]

But that was not the end of it.

---

34. Ironically, the 18 March 1864 issue of *The Princeton Standard* is also missing from the run in several other newspaper collections including Alexander Library, Rutgers, State University of New Jersey; the New Jersey State Library at Trenton; and the Library of Congress, Washington D. C. As recently as ten years ago, Princeton University Library published notification in the New Jersey *Union List of Newspapers* that they owned a paper copy of this issue. When I visited their special collection department in March, 1986, it could not be found.

35. "The New Organ," *Princeton Standard*, Friday, 15 April 1864, p. 2.

36. *Ibid.*

Two weeks later, the newspaper published an editorial, re-markable for its ingenuity:

CORRESPONDENCE OF THE
DAUPHINVILLE COURIER.
Our Organ.

Mr. Editor: – I say it as I would say our youngest has the measles. In fact, the idea once started in our village, the contagion spread until nearly all the young people and many of their elders said resolutely, it must be done; and it was done. Physicians called the prevailing fever, "organ on the brain." All honorable means are used to raise the wind, by gifts, donations, subscriptions, fairs and concerts until sufficient money was collected. A committee of ten of the solidest men in the congregation were appointed to wait upon the largest organ builder in the country and negotiate for the erection of an instru-ment of suitable power and compass. These ten men being [sic], soon secured possession of an organ, which was originally constructed for the Patagonians. — After ominous sounds from the Church of hammer and saw, and diapason, pedal base, flute and trumpet, and many in-goings and out-comings of busy men and curious citi-zens, the public are advertised that the new wonder is ready for exhibition. On the appointed evening behold Dauphinville has gathered at the Church, he beauty and her chivalry as well as strong deputations from the two high schools which flourish here. Audience waiting, chatting, looking, listening in expectation; music-man comes in, all hushed, and the sweet tones of the stop diapason and flute are heard with soft plaintive music. Out comes open diapason, pedal base, principal, trumpet and others successively and the music swells into some grand triumphant symphony. It is a perfect success — audience are delighted — ten solid committee men radiant smiles — (no pun intended Mr. Bibulosity) in short everyone congratulating everybody else upon the fine tone and compass of "our organ." Now comes the rub. Can we allow-a-a-can [*sic*] we allow voluntaries and interludes? Young people say yes. The "grave and reverend seniors" said no. — But I had better give you the result in a form of regulations drawn up by the powers that be.

1. Visitors not allowed to look at the organ unless accompanied with the session and trustees of the Church.

2. The organist not allowed to open the organ except during service or a choir rehearsal, unless in presence of the trustees and session of the Church, or with a written permit from the same.

3. No preludes, interludes, or voluntaries allowed.

4. The organist shall refuse to deliver the key to any visitor, even for a half hour, unless the visitor brings a written order signed by the session and trustees of the Church.

5. The session is ordered to provide slippers for the use of the organist in playing the pedal base.

6. Any infractions of these rules shall be tried by the General Assembly or Court Martial, as the powers direct.

I will add that there is talk of covering the organ with a glass case, or at least a veil of mosquito netting, during the summer season. And also, two lightning rods are to be erected for the further security of the church and its valuable contents. [signed] Suffolk.[37]

Like the uncanny prediction of a clairvoyant, the ultimate irony occurred several weeks later when the building was hit by lightning! The local press reported:

The First Presbyterian Church of this place (Dr. Macdonald's), was struck by lightning on Monday after-

---

37. "Correspondence of the Dauphinville Courier — Our Organ," *Princeton Standard*, Friday, 29 April 1864, p. 2.

George Jardine, organbuilder.

noon last. The charge broke out the ceiling within the building, but expended itself on the outer side and passed off to the ground, doing no material damage to the church, but electrifying several persons who were near the spot – some passing along the street at the moment.[38]

One can only imagine the thoughts that must have entered the minds of everyone connected with the project. On this occasion, the local press — perhaps wisely — opted for silence.

Despite efforts to raise money by the church people, there were still insufficient funds to pay for the organ. A public notice stated:

---

38. *Princeton Standard*, Friday, 10 June 1864, p. 3.

Arthur D. Walbridge, choir director at the First Presbyterian Church in 1863.

FAIR FOR THE ORGAN FUND. — A fair will be held at Mercer Hall, next Wednesday evening, May 11th, commencing at 7 o'clock. Proceeds to be applied to balance of debt on the organ in the First Church.

Contributions of fancy articles and refreshments are solicited. They may be sent to the Hall on Wednesday morning . . .[39]

It was also necessary to find a competent organist. A resolution at a Session meeting states:

Resolved that Elders Alexander, Wright, and Coun-

---

39. "Fair for the Organ Fund," *Princeton Standard*, Friday, 6 May 1864, p. 3.

21

fort(?) be a committee to nominate a person to be organist; and that the same committee recommend rules to be adopted by the Session to control the playing of the organ and for the direction, in general, of the music of the church.[40]

The minutes of the next meeting note:

> The committee appointed on the 14th inst., reported. 1st.-That a majority of the committee nominated Mr. Karl Langlotz for Organist. After a discussion of this part of their report, Mr. Langlotz was duly elected as organist and chorister: services to begin on the 1st Lord's day in April. 2d.-The committee reported four rules for the direction of the organist: which after some modification, were adopted; as follows: —
>
> I. That there be no "voluntaries," except at the close of the services, as the congregation are retiring; and that this be left to the option of the organist.
>
> II. That there be no "interludes," except a brief one, between the last hymn and the doxology.
>
> III. That there be no anthems, chants, or set pieces sung, except such as may be given out by the minister.
>
> IV. That new tunes be cautiously introduced. Elders Counfort [?], Baker, and Wright were appointed a committee to confer with the chorister and organist as to his salary; and also to arrange for the services of some person to blow the bellows of the organ.[41]

The builder of the organ, George Jardine, was an Englishman. He was born in Dartford, Kent, and came to America in 1836 after serving an apprenticeship with Flight & Robson, a celebrated London firm. Several of his sons eventually joined the firm, and it operated until March, 1900, producing well over 1,000 instruments.

---

40. MS, Session Minutes, First Presbyterian Church, Princeton, New Jersey, Monday, 14 March 1864.

41. *Ibid.*, Monday, 21 March 1864.

Jardine organs were competitively priced and stylistically up-to-date.

The town of Princeton during the eighteenth and nineteenth centuries was predominantly Presbyterian. The College of New Jersey (which became Princeton University in 1895 and Princeton Theological Seminary were both founded by Presbyterians. The latter institution retains its strong denominational ties today. By 1850, Princeton had three independent Presbyterian congregations. Both Second Presbyterian Church and Witherspoon Street Presbyterian Church were offspring of the First Church.

While Second Church was not founded until 1847, the need for a more liberal congregation was felt as early as 1832 when disruption occurred over finances, the desire for more informal worship, and staff problems.[42] Of the three local Presbyterian congregations, this group was probably the first to own an organ, though the date and maker are unknown. An archival excavation of local newspapers and church records, held at the Seminary Library, failed to yield any conclusive information. The first building of the Second Church was designed by John Notman, and erected in 1850. Notman was the same architect who designed the Old College Chapel, and as a Philadelphia resident, it is possible that the organs in both buildings were made by a Philadelphia builder.

One item found among the minutes of an 1860 congregational meeting notes, "A vote of thanks was accorded to Prof. Chs. Langlotz for his aid and exertions in behalf of the church."[43] This could have been "thanks" for assistance in buying an organ, as Langlotz later did for the First Church, but no further details are provided.

The organ was definitely in place by the late 1860's, and proof is found in a newspaper notice which coincides with the dedication of the second building. As preparations were nearing completion on

---

42. *Op. cit.*, no. 28, p. 41.
43. MS, Minutes, Congregational Meetings, Second Presbyterian Church, Princeton, New Jersey, 9 June 1860.

Second Presbyterian Church, showing the unidentified organ of circa 1868.

4 December 1868,[44] the local newspaper announced:

> The new edifice of the 2d Pres. Church is to be taken
> possession of next week. The cushions have been ready
> for some time, and the ladies are now engaged in prepar-
> ing the carpets for the isles. [*sic*] The organ box has been
> removed from the old building and placed inside the
> huge "organ box" in the new . . .[45]

According to the clipping, an instrument appears to have been removed from the old building and placed in the new; the excerpt also
implies that the organ received a new case. A copy of a 1912 interior
photograph was published in the *Princeton Packet*, during 1965.[46] It
displays a three-sectional case of Gothic design recessed under an
arch in the back gallery in a style consistent with the date 1868. The
organ is believed to have remained at Scond Presbyterian until 1912
when it was succeeded by a new organ built by the Hall Organ Co.

---

44. Rev. John T. Duffield, *A Discourse on the History of the Second Presbyterian Church of Princeton, N.J.* (Princeton: The Press, 1876).

45. *Princeton Standard*, 27 November 1868, p. 3.

46. *Princeton Packet*, Wednesday, 17 February 1965.

of West Haven, Connecticut, located at the front of the church.[47]

First and Second Presbyterian Churches and Trinity Episcopal Church had organs by 1868. In 1871, the replacing of earlier organs in town began with new instruments which were much larger and more in accord with the changing taste of the time.

---

47. *Ibid.*; there is also a photograph of this instrument with the article.

Chapter II:
Karl A. Langlotz,
The First Notable Organist in Princeton.

In any profession, there are individuals who, because of their special gifts, shine out above their colleagues. Such notables among nineteenth century organists included George W. Morgan (1822-92), George William Warren (1828-1902), and Clarence Eddy (1851-1937), to name but a few. But the fabric of any profession is comprised of average people who have ordinary gifts, and who work on a daily basis, making a competent but unspectacular contribution. Karl Langlotz, the first organist of repute in Princeton, was one of them.

Karl Alexander Christian Langlotz was born 20 June 1834 in what is now present-day East Germany. His father was a professional musician at the Court of Saxony in Meiningen. At the age of five, Karl began to show an affinity for music; he started piano with his father, and violin with Professor Mahr. About the same time, Karl entered school at the Gymnasium Bernhardium, from which he graduated at the age of sixteen.

In 1850, Karl went to Weimar. He worked with Franz Liszt (1811-86), and played in the orchestra for the premiere of Wagner's *Lohengrin* (1850), under Liszt's direction. In 1853, Karl applied for a passport to visit an older sister in the United States. German authorities of his province rejected the application, stating that he could not complete the sojourn in the requested one year period. His older sister was encouraging him by her stories of the many opportunities which awaited him in America. Karl then went to Hamburg with his father and reapplied for a passport. It was issued, and he boarded

Karl Langlotz, Princeton organist.

a ship bound for the United States.

After seven weeks at sea, Karl arrived in New York during 1853. He immediately settled in Philadelphia and established a music studio, supplementing his income by playing the violin for local musical events. He met his first wife, Miss Emma Rae, and they were married there on 10 January 1856.

The following day, the couple moved to Princeton, New Jersey, and took rooms at the Nassau Inn. Considering the plush accommodations the Inn offers today, this description, in Karl's own words, is amusing:

> We had the best rooms the house afforded, which was, to be sure, some comfort to our pride. But we were not greatly pleased with our quarters, owing to the quality and quantity of the furniture. In our parlor was a sofa with three ancient claw feet; two bricks took the place of the fourth, so that the sofa could be used as a rocking chair as well. Two chairs and a two-legged table propped

against the wall completed the equipment.[1]

While the first year, 1853-54, was a great success, the second was not. Karl took a job at a local school, and during the following year only 25 of 75 students returned. About that time, he first became associated with the College, teaching a class on fencing. During the Fall of 1857, Karl became an instructor of German, and was officially listed with the other faculty at the institution.

Any music instruction Langlotz gave during this period was a private arrangement between teacher and pupil. Subsequently, Karl began a collegiate musical organization comprised of about thirty voices, which became known as the Männerchor. After serving as organist in the College Chapel during the late 1850's, Karl became organist at Trinity Church.

In 1859, Langlotz composed music for the text "Old Nassau," which later became a well-known staple of the collegiate song repertory. He continued as an instructor of German and ran a local music studio. In 1864, when the new organ built by George Jardine & Son was installed at the First Presbyterian Church, Karl became the congregation's first organist at an annual salary of $100. On 25 November 1865, Karl's wife Emma died unexpectedly, leaving him four small children: three boys, Karl A., Clifton A., Rae, and one daughter, Emma E. Langlotz.

Karl continued to teach German at the College until 1868, when he entered the Theological Seminary, graduating in 1871. He was licensed by the Presbytery of New Brunswick on 10 April 1872, but he opted to withdraw on 23 April 1877.

In 1872 he married Virginia I. Dunn, and in 1874 the family relocated to Trenton, New Jersey, where Langlotz established a music studio. In 1902 his second wife died. In declining health, Karl was confined to his home in Trenton beginning in 1913. He died on Thanksgiving day, 25 November 1915, and was interred in Princeton Cemetery. He has since been honored by Princeton University and the greater community as the composer of "Old Nassau."

---

1. "The Autobiography of Karl A. Langlotz," *Old Nassau*. New York: Wilford Seymour Conrow, [1905].

Karl Langlotz made a significant contribution to collegiate and ecclesiastical music of Princeton during the period between 1856 and 1874. He served several of the local churches as organist, taught the town youth to play the violin and piano, and made a marked impression on graduates of the college with his German, fencing, and music instruction.

Sources on Karl Langlotz:

"The Autobiography of Karl A. Langlotz," *Old Nassau.* (New York: Wilford Seymour Conrow, [1905]).

"Composer of 'Old Nassau'," *The Princeton Press*, 11 December 1915, p. 3.

"Composer of 'Old Nassau' Ill," *The New York Times*, Sunday, 21 November 1915, II, p. 8.

"Composer of 'Old Nassau' is Dead," *The Philadelphia Ledger*, 25 November 1915.

"Karl A. Langlotz Buried," *The New York Times*, Sunday, 28 November 1915, II, p. 17.

"'Old Nassau' Composer To Be Buried Here," *The Princeton Press*, 27 November 1915, p. 1.

Princeton Alumni Weekly 16, no. 10 (1 Dec., 1915).

"Prof. C. A. Langlotz Dies," *The New York Times*, Friday, 26 November 1915, p. 13.

"University Receives Tablet in Memory of 'Old Nassau' Author," *The Daily Princetonian*, 22 September 1947, p. 4.

Chapter III:
The End of the Nineteenth Century.

Princeton's first "large" and prestigious instrument arrived in 1871, bought for the "old" College Chapel by Henry Clews (1834-1923) of Newark, New Jersey. Clews was a benefactor of the college, and took an interest in the musical and spiritual well-being of the students.

The organ was ordered from Hall & Labagh of New York, and this letter is among that firm's correspondence:

> 11 July 1870
>
> Mr. J. C. Pennington
> 692 High Street
> Newark.
>
> Enclosed we beg leave to hand you [a] scheme for the organ for [the] Chapel of Princeton College and Memorandum of Agreem[t] for building the same — be pleased to get the signature of the President and return one of the copies to us.
>
> [unsigned, Hall][1]

A follow-up communication states:

> J. C. Pennington   26th Oct[r] 1870
> Your's of the 24th Ins[t] addressed to our Mr. [James] Kemp [1827-91] has been duly received. We cannot now state with positive certainty what day we shall be ready to send on the Organ. Circumstances beyond our control have conspired to retard our operations, and we [are]

---

1. MS, Hall & Labagh Correspondence, v. II, p. 233.

First Presbyterian Church, showing the 1875 Jardine organ (previous page). John C. Pennington, college student and organist (above). Programme of Exhibition for the 1871 Hall & Labagh organ in the Old College Chapel (right).

constrain^d to say that it will be a month beyond the time specified in the contract before we shall be able to place the Organ in your chapel. We are exceedingly sorry for this delay, but as before mentioned, it has been out of our power to avoid it.

[unsigned, Hall][2]

In the meantime, Hall lent to the college a small organ which he probably made about 1820. According to an article in *The Diapason*, "this organ was lent . . . until the firm could finish the building of a new organ. For some years afterwards it was on Governor's Island, in New York harbor, where it was used by General Hancock and his

2. *Ibid.*, p. 251.

GRAND CONCERT

AND

 rgan Exhibition!

IN

PRINCETON COLLEGE CHAPEL,

Tuesday Evening, Jan. 17th, 1871.

The following are the performers on this occasion:

Mr. W. A. M. Diller,

Organist of St. Mary's Church, Brooklyn.

Mr. Jos. P. Pennington,

Mr. J. C. Pennington,

ORGANISTS.

THE BEETHOVEN QUARTETTE,

CONSISTING OF

Mr. COHEN, 1st Violin and Soloist,

Mr. HINDS, 2d Violin,

Mr. WARD, Pianist,

Mr. FARREL, Violincello.

The Organ was presented to the College by Mr Henry Clews, of New York, and was built by Messrs. Hall, Labagh & Co., of New York.

Doors open at 7¼ P. M.   Concert to commence at 8.

Ward & Tichenor, Printers, 832 Broad Street, Newark, N. J.

33

PART I.

1. MARCH—From "The Prophet,"   .   .   *Meyerbeer*

    Mr. J. C. PENNINGTON.

2. SELECTIONS— Don Giovanni,   .   .   .   *Mozart*

    BEETHOVEN QUARTETTE.

3. LARGHETTO—From 2d Symphony,   .   .   *Beethoven*

    Mr. JOS. P. PENNINGTON.

4. VIOLIN SOLO—7th Air Varie,   .   .   *De Beriot*

    Mr. COHEN.

5. OFFERTOIRE IN G, ...   *Wely*

    Mr. W. A. M. DILLER.

6. "BEATRICE,"   .   .   .   .   .   .   *De Beriot*

    BEETHOVEN QUARTETTE.

Programme.

PART II.

1. ADAGIO SONATA PATHETIQUE,   .   *Beethoven*

   Mr. J. C. PENNINGTON.

2. VIOLIN SOLO—" Il Trovatore,"   .   .   .   . *Alard*

   Mr. COHEN.

3. RONDOLETTO SPOHR OP 49—Arranged for Organ by

                                        Diller

   Mr. W. A. M. DILLER.

4. " ANNA BOLENA,"   .   .   .   .   . *De Beriot*

   BEETHOVEN QUARTETTE.

5. OVERTURE—William Tell, ... *Rossini*

   Mr. W. A. M. DILLER.

William Augustus Muhlenberg Diller, organist (above). The 1871 Hall &
Labagh organ in the Old College Chapel (right).

wife, both lovers of organ music."[3] Later, it was erected in the
residence of Joseph M. Priaulx, son-in-law of James Kemp, and
ultimately, it was given to Vassar College by Walter M. Mohr (d.
1955) who had a daughter educated there. The organ is still at Vassar
College today, dismantled and awaiting restoration.

According to the financial records of Princeton College, the
cost of the new Hall & Labagh organ, paid by 18 January 1871, was
$2,579.25, not including $26.50 for freight to have the organ shipped
from New York. Henry Clews contributed $2,275.00,[4] slightly
shy of the total, which the College raised by selling the Hartwick
organ.

The public exhibition took place on Tuesday evening, 17 January 1871, and featured William Augustus Muhlenberg Diller (1836-
80),[5] then organist of St. Mary's Church in Brooklyn, Joseph Pope

---

3. "Residence Organ of Century Ago for Vassar Museum," *The Diapason* v. 23,
no. 7 (1 June 1932): 23.
4. MS, Financial Ledger, Princeton College, "Organ Fund."
5. W. A. M. Diller was born in Brooklyn in 1836, and was named after his

Pennington (1846-1926), and John C. Pennington (1850-97). Diller played an *Offertoire* by Lefébure-Wély, the Overture to *William Tell* by Rossini, and a piece of his own composition. The spotlight was shared with the Beethoven String Quartet.[6]

In 1880, a new chapel building was given to the college by Henry Gurdon Marquand (1819-1902) of New York, and by May, 1882 the structure was nearing completion. The Hall & Labagh organ of 1871 which had served in the previous chapel was relocated to the new building. Said the local paper: "The organ in the chapel was removed during the week to the Marquand Chapel. A reed organ is used in the meantime."[7] In order to make the appearance of the organ congruous with the architecture of the edifice, a new case

renowned grandfather, The Rev. Dr. Muhlenberg. He showed an astonishing incli-
nation toward music and held a post as church organist by the time he was twelve.
According to Albert H. Messiter, "Without being a great player, he handled the
organ with much skill, and often produced fine effects in his accompaniments." In
1865 he became the assistant organist of Trinity Church, New York, resigning that
charge in 1866 because of stress. He was later organist of St. Mary's Episcopal
Church, Brooklyn (which owned an important Reuben Midmer organ installed in
1870), and other Brooklyn churches. He died in 1880 at the age of 47. For more detail
see A. H. Messiter, *A History of the Choir and Music of Trinity Church, New York From
its Organization, to the Year 1897.* (New York: Edwin S. Gorham, Publisher, 1906), p.
112-113.

6. *Grand Concert and Organ Exhibition in the Princeton College Chapel, Tuesday
Evening, Jan. 17th, 1871.*

7. *Princeton Press,* Saturday, 13 May 1882, p. 2.

1871 Hall & Labagh organ in the Old College Chapel (left). The exterior of Marquand Chapel (above). The interior of Marquand Chapel, showing the 1871 Hall & Labagh organ with a new case (below).

was designed and provided. We do not know who did the work.

The Hall & Labagh of 1871 functioned in Marquand Chapel for another fifteen years. Then, the college daily opined:

> The condition of the Chapel organ is such that a proper chapel service is almost, if not quite, an impossibility. We who are here realize this much more fully than is possible for the alumni and for this reason we would like to make a plea to them for a new organ. The old one has served us long and well but the days of its usefulness are past; for something like twenty-five years it has seen constant service and no wonder it groans in seeming agony at being compelled to continue its labor of love. It never was supplied with proper stops for chapel singing and those that it once had, are worn and broken till they no longer perform their duties. The whole organ in fact is so completely played out that it is impossible to repair it.
>
> A new organ is absolutely essential to the betterment of the chapel exercises, which for the last few months, we can almost say years, have been greatly handicapped by poor music . . . We learn that a committee has this matter in charge and have succeeded in raising about one-half the amount necessary to purchase an organ, the remainder we feel sure would be most gladly contributed by the alumni could they but fully appreciate the disgraceful condition of the present organ which cannot be repaired.[8]

One month later, there was an outright solicitation:

A NEW ORGAN FOR MARQUAND CHAPEL

Princeton, N. J., April 26, 1896.

Editor of *The Alumni Princetonian*:

May I take advantage of your columns to appeal to

---

8. *The Daily Princetonian*, Wednesday, 24 March 1897, p.2.

the alumni to help the subscription toward a new organ for the Marquand Chapel. The present organ, as all know, is nearly worn out. It cannot be repaired to advantage. Many of the pipes have been shut off because of their discordant sounds. The part of the organ which can still be played is difficult to keep in any tune. Several times the instrument has broken down while being used in the chapel services and last Sunday morning it collapsed during the second hymn. A new organ of proper size and quality will cost $4500. $3000 has already been pledged in the way of subscriptions and $300 will be allowed on the old organ, leaving $1200 still to raise. This ought to be raised without delay. If college is to open next fall with a new organ in place of the old one, the new instrument must be ordered early in May at the latest. Will not the alumni co-operate and send in subscriptions of $5, $10, and $20, or even $50, to make up the $1,200 needed? Such subscriptions may be sent directly to E[dwin]. C[urtis]. Osborn [1850-1901], Treasurer of Princeton University.

Andrew E. West.[9]

The funds were quickly raised and by early August the organ was being installed. Built by Müller & Abel of New York, it had two manuals and 35 speaking and mechanical registers.[10] A detailed description of the instrument, including its stoplist, is published in the appendix to this book.

Oscar Müller and George Abel were both employees of the famous Roosevelt brothers. When the Roosevelt Organ Works closed in 1893, the two men formed a partnership under their own name, known as Müller & Abel, and commenced building organs in 1894. They issued an elaborate catalogue which described a series of standard-sized instruments, much like the catalogues published by

9. "A New Organ For Marquand Chapel," *The Alumni Princetonian*, 29 April 1897, p.2.
10. "New Organ in Marquand Chapel," *Princeton Press*, Saturday, 7 August 1897, p. 2.

*The interior of Marquand Chapel, showing the organ built by Müller &
Abel in 1897 (above). A Müller & Abel advertisement (below).*

the Roosevelts. Despite their reputation for high-quality organs,
they appear to have been poor businessmen and went bankrupt in
1903 after making about 60 instruments. One of their last organs
was built for the congregation of Zion German Lutheran Church,
Henry Street, in Brooklyn, New York. Still extant, this instrument
illustrates both their good reputation for quality and their attention
to detail.

 A subsequent report at Princeton University described some of

the changes made during summer vacation. In addition to mentioning the new Müller & Abel organ, it documented disposition of the old one:

> Last, but not least, is the new pipe organ in Marquand Chapel, the gift of a number of interested alumni at a cost of over $5,000 . . . The old chapel organ, after its long service here, has gone to a Bowery Mission in New York City.[11]

The twentieth century organ historian, Frederick R. Webber (1887-1963), examined the organ at the Mission. He wrote:

> The console is attached to the C end of the organ. The organ, with a rather handsome front, stands in a gallery above a preaching platform. The stops have round shanks, a long draw, and bulbous, oblique discs, facing the organist. The engraving is Old English, Mason & Hamlin harmonium style of lettering. Front pipes are rather slender, and neatly made . . .[12]

The old organ remained at the Mission until the mid 1970s when it was removed by the Organ Clearing House. Parts of the instrument were incorporated into an essentially new organ built by the Stuart Organ Co., of Aldenville, Massachusetts, Opus 10 (1976), for the United Methodist Church, Sudbury, Massachusetts.[13]

The new Müller & Abel organ in Marquand Chapel was not heard in public recital until later that Fall. The *Alumni Princetonian* reported:

> On last Saturday evening an organ recital was given in Marquand Chapel by Mr. [Henry Clay] Briggs [1872-1964], the University organist.[14] This was the first

---

11. "Vacation Changes," *Princeton Press*, Saturday, 18 September 1897, p. 2.
12. MS, Frederick R. Webber, stoplist collection.
13. *Dedicatory Recital Program*, Sudbury United Methodist Church, Sudbury, Massachusetts, 14 November 1976. The Stuart Organ Co., Opus 10 (1976).
14. Henry Clay Briggs was born in Brooklyn, New York, on 4 May 1872. He studied music at Columbia Conservatory of Music and later became an organ student of George W. Morgan from 1888 to 1892. He entered Princeton University in 1892 and graduated in 1896, when he immediately entered Princeton Theological Semi-

Henry Clay Briggs, college organist.

chance that the undergraduates and public have had of listening to the many powers and capabilities of the new organ, which was placed in the chapel during the past summer . . . A large and interesting audience listened to a very attractive program . . . rendered in a very pleasing style.[15]

Notable works on the program included the *Toccata and Fugue in D minor* and the *Prelude and Fugue in C Major* of J. S. Bach, and the *Triumphal March* of Alexandre Guilmant. The article described some of the performances and concluded by publishing the program.

The organ had tubular-pneumatic playing action, and was installed in a divided location on opposite sides of the chancel, forty-five feet apart.[16] Tubular-pneumatic action was still relatively new, and not all types were completely reliable. According to the newspaper, some of the lead tubes were 55 feet long, and within ten years, the organ was nearly unplayable. The minutes of a trustees' meeting

---

nary, finishing that program in 1899. Beginning in 1897, he served the University as organist and choirmaster.

15. "Organ Recital," *The Alumni Princetonian*, 18 November 1897, p.7.

16. *Princeton Press*, Saturday, 7 August 1897, p. 2.

at the University in 1907 lament:

> The organ in Marquand Chapel, built by Müller &
> Able [sic] in 1897, at a cost of $4350.35, is in very bad
> condition. It requires an entire new action, the cost of
> which will be nearly equal to the purchase of a new
> organ.[17]

By this time, the firm was out of business. Minutes of a later meeting
record:

> On account of the condition of the organ in Mar-
> quand Chapel, which cannot possibly last throughout
> the year, it is found necessary to either install an entire
> new action with chests or consider the purchase of a new
> organ. Estimates have been received from E. O. Odell &
> Co. [sic], [Hook &] Hastings Co., and the Hutchings-
> Votey Organ Co. for the necessary repairs on this organ
> and it will cost from $3,000 to $3500.[18]

Because there is no evidence that the college purchased a new
organ, it seems likely that the Müller & Abel was rebuilt, though
which firm did the work is not certain. The fairly complete account
ledger of J.H. & C.S. Odell from the period, preserved in the American Organ Archive,[19] makes no mention of such a project, and it is
not listed by Hook & Hastings.

Ultimately, the organ had a swift demise when Marquand
Chapel was destroyed by fire on Friday, 14 May 1920. The local
paper bemoaned:

> From late reports of the loss resulting from the fire last
> Friday evening, which destroyed Dickenson Hall and
> Marquand Chapel, it is evident that Princeton University

---

17. MS, Trustee Minutes, Princeton University, 14 March 1907.
18. Ibid., 10 June 1907.
19. While it is likely that J.H. & C.S. Odell did not rebuild the action, they did
have responsibility for tuning and general maintenance of the organ. Their account
ledger shows entries beginning on 28 December 1906, and continuing on a regular
basis until 15 September 1913. Thereafter is a notice which states, "Continued New
Ledger, page 78." See MS, Account Ledger, J. H. & C.S. Odell, p. 150-151.

Geo. Jardine & Son,

ORGAN BUILDERS,

318 & 320 E. 39th St.

BET. 1ST AND 2D AVENUES,   *NEW YORK CITY.*

The Jardine factory, about 1890.

suffers a loss in art treasures that can never be replaced . . . stained glass windows, and the organ were particularly valuable . . .[20]

A new chapel was eventually built, and it houses one of Ernest M. Skinner's favorite organs, Opus 656 (1927).[21]

During the last years of the nineteenth century, Princeton University acquired an instrument built by George Jardine & Son for Alexander Hall, and this organ also had tubular-pneumatic action.[22] The stoplist and a brief description were published in *The Musical Opinion*, (an unlikely source because it was published in England), and it is transcribed in the appendix of this book.

An early notice of the organ appeared in the gossip column of the *Princeton Press*: "Workmen are engaged in putting a large organ in Alexander Hall. It will occupy the gallery where the band has been stationed on commencement occasions."[23] Two weeks later, the same publication stated, "The new organ in Alexander Hall is completed. Yesterday, an organist gave an exhibition of its quality to a tolerable number of persons."[24]

The University newspaper also noticed the instrument in an article titled, "Improvements in Alexander Hall:"

> By far the greatest addition is the new two-manual pipe organ at the end of the gallery on the speaker's right, which is a gift by Mrs. [Charles B.] Alexander.[25]

The inaugural recital was not held until almost two years later, on Thursday evening, 21 April 1898:

> The first public recital on the new organ in Alexander Hall will be given this evening at 8 o'clock by Mr. Harold Bond Nason '98 [1877-1951], assisted by Mr.

---

20. *The Princeton Packet*, 21 May 1920, p. 1.
21. "The Skinner and Aeolian-Skinner Opus List," *The Boston Organ Club Newsletter* v. 8, no.9 (November, 1972): 3.
22. *Musical Opinion and Music Trade Review* (1 October, 1896): 25.
23. *Princeton Press*, Saturday, 22 August 1896, p. 3.
24. *Ibid.*, Saturday, 5 September 1896, p. 3.
25. "Improvements in Alexander Hall," *The Daily Princetonian*, Wednesday, 7 October 1896, p. 1.

The Jardine crew, about 1890 (above). The interior of Alexander Hall, showing the 1896 Jardine organ (right).

William Gillespie of the University, under the auspices of the Philadelphian Society.

Mr. Nason is the organist of the First Presbyterian Church, Germantown, Philadelphia, and was formerly a pupil of Alexandre Guilmant, of Paris.[26]

---

26. "Organ Recital," *The Daily Princetonian*, Thursday, 21 April 1898, p. 1.

The interior of Alexander Hall, showing the 1896 Jardine organ.

The program included works by Berthold Tours, Alphonse Mailly, Arthur Sullivan, N. J. Lemmens, as well as by Guilmant. A brief review in the *Daily Princetonian* stated:

> An appreciative audience attended the organ recital given by Mr. H. B. Nason '98, in Alexander Hall last evening, for the benefit of the Philadelphian Society. The Selections by Mr. Nason were beautifully rendered and

Mr. Gillespie's solo also received a great deal of applause.

This was the first public recital which has thus far been given on the new organ in Alexander Hall.[27]

The author had the privilege of playing this organ in the fall of 1974 while it sat decaying in the corner of the balcony of Alexander Hall. I recall the elegance of the flute registers and the large scale of the Great Open Diapason. The organ was in very poor condition. After the opinions of several competent musicians were sought (the author not among them), plans were made to dispose of the organ during 1986. As of this writing, those plans have not been carried out, and the organ is still in place. Though substantially rebuilt, it is the last Princeton organ surviving from the nineteenth century.

By the last quarter of the century, several area churches also boasted new instruments. Trinity Episcopal Church replaced the one-manual Hall & Labagh organ with a new instrument built by J.H. & C.S. Odell, Opus 111 (1872).[28] Recorded in the minutes of the vestry during October 1871 is:

The subject of a New Organ was then discust [sic] and taken up & the following resolutions adopted:

Resolved, that there be a committee appointed to dispose of the Old Organ to the best advantage, & purchase a new organ. The Chair appointed Joseph C. Eden, J. D. Lippincott, R. S. Conover, Rev. S. B. Baker, "Committee."[29]

At two other meetings, the organ was briefly discussed. but the only record in the minutes was "Committee on Organ reported progress."[30]

The congregation of Trinity Episcopal Church had moved to a larger edifice dedicated two years earlier on 7 June 1870.[31] The 1850

---

27. "Organ Recital," *The Daily Princetonian*, Friday, 22 April 1898, p. 4.

28. MS, J.H. & C.S. Odell Opus List. Compiled by F. R. Webber.

29. MS, Vestry Minutes, Trinity Episcopal Church, Princeton, New Jersey, 23 October 1871.

30. *Ibid.*, 13 November 1871, and 4 March 1872.

31. Margery P. Cuyler and Nathanial Burt, *The History of Trinity Church, Princeton, New Jersey: 1833-1914.* (Published by the Church), p. 194.

A J.H. & C.S. Odell advertisement from 1861 (left). Henry Stephen Cutler, organist of Trinity Church in New York (above).

Hall & Labagh organ was too small to lead congregational singing in the larger building, and a campaign for a new instrument was initiated. In May, 1872, the local press announced:

> The new organ of Trinity Church, will be opened, at a special service, on Tuesday evening, May 21st, at half past seven o,clock. Dr. H[enry]. S[tephen]. Cutler [1824-1902], will preside at the organ, and the choir of Christ Church, New York, will assist in the musical part of the service. The public are invited.[32]

Two brothers, John Henry Odell (1830-99) and Caleb Sherwood Odell (1827-93) formed their business in 1859 after serving their indenture with Richard M. Ferris (1818-58). They were im-

---

32. *The Princetonian*, Saturday, 18 May 1872, p. 3.

The console of the 1872 J.H. & C.S. Odell organ in Trinity Church (above). The facade of the 1872 J.H. & C.S. Odell organ in Trinity Church (right).

mediately successful, and during the year 1865 alone built fifteen organs. Of the prominent nineteenth-century organbuilding shops in New York, the Odell firm was the longest to survive: the company continued to manufacture new organs until 1959, a century after its formation.

Frederick R. Webber, who personally examined records of J.H.

& C.S. Odell, transcribed the stoplist from factory archives while the firm was still in business.[33] The Odell served Trinity Church until it was replaced by a four manual instrument built by the Austin Organ Co., of Hartford, Connecticut, Opus 775 (1917).[34]

First Presbyterian Church acquired a new instrument in 1875 from George Jardine & Son, of New York. Less information is available on it than on any other organ installed in Princeton during the late nineteenth century. The organ was acquired as part of a major interior renovation project, and received almost no press notice. One brief item stated:

> OPENING OF THE CHURCH. — The First Church was opened last Friday evening to the public by the committee who have had in charge its enlargement, beautifying, and repairs . . . the organ has been removed to a recess in the rear of the pulpit . . .[35]

While session and trustee minutes of the church are also silent on the installation, a history notes, "A second and larger Jardine organ was set up in the recess back of the pulpit in 1875 or not long after . . ."[36]

Concomitantly, the 1864 organ by Jardine, which had served for only eleven years, was relocated to the Witherspoon Street Church, the third Presbyterian congregation in Princeton. This church had its foundation going back to a fire which destroyed the First Church on 6 July 1835.[37] Apparently, white members of the congregation were cordially invited to worship at the chapel of Princeton Theological Seminary, but the same courtesy was not extended to black worshipers. This and some misunderstandings led to the formal organization of a new church on 4 September 1840.[38]

---

33. *Op. cit.*, no. 12.

34. *A List of Organs Installed by Austin Organ Company, Hartford, Conn.* ([Hartford, Connecticut]: Published by the firm, 1919).

35. "Opening of the Church," *Princeton Press*, 12 June 1875, p. 3.

36. Charles G. Osgood, *The First Church.* (Princeton: [Published by the Church], 1937), p. 15.

37. Arthur S. Link, *The First Presbyterian Church of Princeton: Two Centuries of History.* (Princeton, New Jersey: The First Presbyterian Church, 1967), p. 61.

38. John Frelinghuysen Hageman, *History of Princeton and Its Institutions . . .* (Philadelphia: J. B. Lippincott & Co., 1879), p. 210.

The 1875 Geo. Jardine & Son organ in First Presbyterian Church.

Sarah Harris, a local resident and life-long member of the Witherspoon Street Church, recalled the Jardine organ. She told the author:

> My mother, Margaret Van Zant Blackwell [1875–1959], played the organ at the Witherspoon Church for 42 years, retiring in 1940. The organ was located at the front of the church and had two sets of keys. During the early years it was still hand-pumped and mother used her nephew as the bellows boy. When mother retired, I took over as organist, and served for 38 years until 1978 . . .[39]

The 1864 organ served the Witherspoon Street congregation from 1875 until 1922, when it was replaced by M. P. Möller, Opus 3274 (1922), a 2-17.[40] Following its service there, a history of the First Church states the organ was "reclaimed [in 1922] by our organist, Mr. Morriset, in whose house it now stands, sweetly vocal and reminiscent of other days."[41] The ultimate fate of this organ is unknown.

39. Phone conversation with the author, March, 1986.
40. *List of More Than 5400 Möller Pipe Organs, 1880–1928.* (Hagerstown, Maryland: M. P. Möller Co., 1928).
41. *Op. cit.*, no. 36.

Saint Paul's R. C. Church was founded about 1850, and the congregation immediately erected a small stone building. By 1870, a third edifice had been built, and the pastor, Rev. T. P. Moran, bought second-hand for $225 the 1860 Hartwick organ which had served in the chapel at the College of New Jersey. When the time came to replace the instrument in 1917 with a new C.S. Haskell organ built in Philadelphia, the newspaper reported:

> The new organ will replace the old historical instrument which the church obtained from Princeton University years ago. This old organ was purchased in 1876 [*sic*, 1870] and it was the first [*sic*, 1860] organ used at the University in the old chapel. The organ is for sale, but several residents here are agitating a movement to raise enough money to purchase the instrument and keep it in Princeton as one of the historical relics. The organ could be placed in the University and kept there with the many other historical relics which have been gathered.[42]

Despite the plea, the organ is not known to be preserved.

The Methodist Episcopal Church was organized in 1845, and its first building was erected during 1847.[43] There is no indication that the congregation owned or used an organ before 1870, when the local newspaper noted:

> ORGAN FUND CONCERT. — The concert to be given in aid of the Organ Fund Association, in the Methodist Episcopal Church of our place, on Tuesday evening next, will be well worthy of the patronage of the public. The performers are not professionals . . . The lovers of good music and the friends of the Organ Fund Association ought to crowd the Church to its utmost capacity on Tuesday night next.[44]

Both the date of installation and maker remain unknown.

---

42. "New Pipe Organ for St. Paul's," *Princeton Press*, 31 August 1917, p. 6.
43. *Op. cit.*, no 38, p. 195.
44. "Organ Fund Concert," *Princeton Standard*, Friday, 18 March 1870, p. 3.

One other late nineteenth-century organ was installed in Princeton in the chapel of the Theological Seminary. A careful scrutiny of historical records at the Seminary has uncovered only the information that the organ was rebuilt in 1919 by the Haskell company of Philadelphia.

By 1885, all of the local churches had organs. The practice of the wealthier congregations replacing their organs as soon as style shifted was already well-established. By the turn of the century, yet another round of bigger and even more notable instruments displaced their precursors. The First Presbyterian Church took the lead just after the turn of the century, and the Town of Princeton acquired its first three-manual organ.

An artist's rendition of the 1902 Hillgreen, Lane & Co. organ in the First Presbyterian Church. Despite the central location of the instrument in the illustration, the organ was always located at the side of the sanctuary.

Chapter IV:
A New Century.

The George Jardine & Son organ of 1875 in the First Church was used until it was replaced in 1902 with a new instrument, Opus 28, built by Hillgreen, Lane, & Co., of Alliance, Ohio.[1] According to church histories, this organ was the gift of Mr. & Mrs. William M. Paxton as a memorial to their son, Harmon Denny Paxton (d. 1896).[2] It was larger than the Jardine and had three manuals.

Hillgreen, Lane & Co. had been in business only a short time when the contract was signed. The firm was headed by a partnership comprised of Alfred Hillgreen (1859-1923), a native of Sweden, and Charles Alva Lane (1854-1933), and was established in 1898. A circa 1905 catalogue proudly described the high-quality materials from which Hillgreen, Lane & Co. organs were constructed:

> The interior Key-desk work is made of Mahogany, unless otherwise stipulated. The keys are of the best Ivory and Ebony, while all the Stop Knob Faces, Piston Buttons, Coupler Tablets, etc., are of Ivory, hand-engraved and lettered.
>
> In the construction of the Wood Pipes we use only the high-grade Pine, and this enters into other parts of the work, no cheap lumber whatever being employed.
>
> Our metal and zinc pipes are usually heavy, especially in the Diapason work. All the "composition metal" is rich in Tin, some of the "string stops" consisting of pure Tin.

---

1. MS, Hillgreen-Lane, *Factory Opus List*, courtesy of Robert Hillgreen, Jr.
2. Charles G. Osgood, *The First Church*. (Princeton: [Published by the Church]), p. 16.

Alfred Hillgreen, organbuilder.

Owing to the refined and characteristic voicing of our instruments tone-experts have everywhere given us enthusiastic praise. One Organist has said: "Your Diapason tones hold dreams of Old-World Cathedrals, while in your string work one can almost smell resin." The nobility of tone noted in the fundamental stops of our organs is obtained by the use of the most generous scales and unstinted metal-sheets. The Reed stops, which are also made under our direct supervision, are marvelously accurate imitations of the instruments whose "proxies" they bear in the tonal composition of the Organ.

To all matters of detail we give watchful attention and ceaseless study. Just here it may be said, it is a maxim in our experimental department that mechanical simplicity must always take preference over either pneumatic or electrical treatment where alternatives are presented. Patrons may therefore feel assured of the utmost dependableness in the "Action" of our instruments, knowing that, so far as possible, the hazards of both pneumatic and electrics have been eliminated . . .[3]

The earliest press coverage of the Princeton installation reported: "The builders are removing the old organ and installing the new one in the First Presbyterian Church."[4] Complications immediately arose because the Hillgreen, Lane & Co. organ was so much larger than the Jardine. The next issue stated:

> The work of installing the new organ in the First Presbyterian Church will take considerable time. The question of location having finally been determined it is necessary to make room for the instrument by taking a portion of the pastor's room and the room above. Owing to these alterations the Easter morning services of the congregation will be held to-morrow in the Marquand Chapel.[5]

An issue early in May noted: "Hillgreen, Lane & Co. have spared no pains to make it a perfect up-to-date instrument, with the latest mechanical devices and improvements. The instrument has been passed by the experts employed by the trustees as perfect both in materials and workmanship . . ."[6]

The opening recital took place on Thursday evening, 8 May 1902, at 8:15 p.m. The local paper reported:

> ORGAN RECITAL. The organ recital at the First Church on Thursday evening was attended by a very large audience. The recital was in charge of Mr. Francis Cuyler Van Dyck, Jr. [1873-1916], and he was assisted by Edwin H. Kellogg 1902, organist of the First Church, Mrs. Mary Dunn Kaser, soprano, and Mr. Robert

3. *Hillgreen-Lane Organs: Churches, Halls, and Residences. Factories, Alliance, Ohio.* (Cleveland, Ohio: L. S. & B. Illustrating Co., [1905?]).
4. *Princeton Press*, Saturday, 22 March 1902, p. 4.
5. *Ibid.*, Saturday, 29 March 1902, p. 6.
6. "First Church Organ," *Princeton Press*, Saturday, 3 May 1902, p. 4.

Hosea, baritone, of the Fifth Avenue Presbyterian Church of New York City. The organ stands on the left of the pulpit recess as you enter the church, and is a fine specimen of ecclesiastical architecture. The mechanism of the instrument . . . includes all the most modern improvements in the noblest of musical instruments. The exhibition on Thursday evening fulfilled the expectations of the builders and the congregation. The parts of the organ are well balanced, and its possibilities for interpreting musical compositions are unusual . . .[7]

The article went on to cite performers and acclaim the program which included the *First Sonata* of Felix Mendelssohn, the *Fugue in D* of J. S. Bach, and the popular "O Divine Redeemer" of Charles Gounod.[8]

Van Dyck was delighted with the instrument, and wrote a letter of testimonial to the firm which they published in their circa 1905 catalogue.[9] He noted:

Every facility was afforded me by the Builders to examine the work, both during the installation of the instrument and after its completion. After a most careful study I am prepared to say the instrument is satisfactory in every particular. As to tone, I can only say I am more than pleased. Better flutes I have never heard; indeed, all classes of stops show a refinement and individuality of voicing that is unusual. Altogether, the instrument is a success, and is evidence of your wisdom in selecting your builder from the list of the very few scientific and artistic craftsmen of this country.

Francis Cuyler Van Dyck, Jr., Princeton, N. J.[10]

Like the recently installed Müller & Abel organ of 1897 in the

---

7. *Ibid.*, Saturday, 10 May 1902, p. 4.
8. *Ibid.*
9. "Francis Cuyler Van Dyck," *The Diapason* v. 7, no. 4 (1 March 1916): 8.
10. *Hillgreen-Lane Organs: Churches, Halls, and Residences. Factories, Alliance, Ohio.* (Cleveland, Ohio: L.S. & B. Illustrating Co., [1905?]), testimonials.

The 1902 Hillgreen, Lane & Co. organ, shown in a photograph after the console was relocated to the rear gallery of the church.

College Chapel, and the George Jardine & Son organ of 1896 in Alexander Hall, the Hillgreen, Lane & Co. organ at the First Church had tubular-pneumatic action, and unfortunately, such mechanisms were not trouble-free. By 1914, the organ required renovations costing $5,000,[11] and the work was probably done by the Hall Organ Company, of New Haven, Connecticut. "First Presbyterian Church, Princeton, N.J.," is found on their *Classified List*.[12] In 1941, the organ was again rebuilt. It was fitted with a new console located in the rear gallery of the church,[13] and had tonal revisions. The congregation used the organ until it was replaced with a new instrument made by Walter Holtkamp, of Cleveland, Ohio, Opus 1721 (1959).[14]

Another interesting old organ appeared in the gallery of the First Church during 1944. A history states:

> On September 24, 1944, Dr. John Finlay [*sic*] Williamson
> [1887-1964] donated a small organ to the church which is
> "believed to be the first to be used in the present structure."
> In 1948 this organ was installed in the balcony beside the
> large console.[15]

According to Barbara Owen, who was a student in Princeton during the 1950s, the organ was a small one-manual George Jardine organ dating from about the middle of the nineteenth century. Because we know the first organ at the church had two manuals, this could not have been the same instrument. Its current whereabouts is not known.

During the second decade of the twentieth century, several institutions purchased other new instruments. Second Presbyterian Church acquired an organ built H. Hall & Co. of New Haven, Connecticut, during 1912. It was installed at the front of the room,

---

11. Arthur S. Link, *The First Presbyterian Church: Two Centuries of History*. (Princeton, New Jersey: The First Presbyterian Church, 1967), p. 89.

12. *Classified List of Hall Organs*. (West Haven, Connecticut: The Hall Organ Company, [1928?]).

13. *Op. cit.*, no. 11, p. 97.

14. John Allen Ferguson, *Walter Holtkamp: American Organ Builder*. ([Kent. Ohio]: The Kent State University Press, [1979]), p. 139.

15. *Op. cit.*, no. 11, p. 98.

The 1912 Hall & Co. organ in the Second Presbyterian Church (above). A later building of the Hall Organ Company (below).

and the stoplist was printed in *The Diapason*.[16] It is believed to have been the first organ in town with electro-pneumatic playing action.

The local newspaper announced the opening:

> On Monday evening, March 18 [1912], at 8 o'clock, an organ recital will be given on the new organ in the Second Presbyterian Church by Professor Francis Cuyler Van Dyck, Jr., of Lawrenceville, with Miss Marie Stoddart, of New York, as soloist. — The public is cordially invited to be present.[17]

16. "Build for Princeton, N.J.," *The Diapason* v. 3, no. 3 (1 February 1912): 1.
17. "Organ Recital," *Princeton Press*, 16 March 1912, p. 1.

It was an unbelievable success, and even the large Second Church was "too small to accommodate the great crowd . . . gathered . . . to hear the first public recital."[18]

The article went on to describe the organ:

> In tonal effects, as well as in perfection of workmanship, the organ is a great credit to the donor and to the builders, Messrs. H. Hall and Company of New Haven. The instrument is of electro-pneumatic action throughout, and has a full equipment of pipes in the great organ, the swell and the pedal organ, together with a large complement of couplers, combination pistons and pedal movements. Its accessories include the swell tremolo, wind indicator, a five horse power Century motor, which furnished two pressures of wind; and an electric generator for action. The massive gothic case was designed by Mr. L. W. Robinson of New Haven and gives the instrument a very handsome setting.[19]

This organ remained in use until 1967 when it was rebuilt by George Kritikos, who had been trained and employed by the Walcker Organ Company in Germany, and who operated his own organ building firm in Brazil for thirty years before immigrating to the United States. The organ was removed in 1988 and the parts sold to various individuals and churches.

In 1916, a large Aeolian Organ of four manuals was installed in Procter Hall at the Princeton Graduate College, and the original contract for the instrument is published in this book. It was the gift of Henry Clay Frick (1849-1919), and cost over $40,000, an enormous amount for the time. It had a spectacular case located in the rear gallery of the dining commons designed in part by architect Ralph Adams Cram.[20] Following its installation, a recital series was established, which in its first season scheduled fifteen performances. A war-time coal shortage interrupted the series mid-stream in January

---

18. "Large Crowd . . .," *Princeton Press*, 23 March 1912, p. 2.
19. *Ibid.*
20. MS, Contract.

The exterior of the Princeton Graduate College (previous page). Detail of the 1916 Aeolian Co. case in Procter Hall (above). The same case in a photograph taken shortly after the installation (right).

of 1917. During the subsequent decade, the series featured many famous organists, including J. Frederick Wolle (1863-1933), founder of the Bethlehem Bach Choir, and Marcel Dupré (1886-1971), organist of St. Sulpice in Paris. G. Alexander Russell (1880-1953), an organist and Princeton faculty member, was responsible for the series.

The Aeolian Company was celebrated primarily for the construction of residence instruments. The organ department of the firm was established about the turn of the century, and it remained in business until 1932, when it merged with the Skinner Organ Company to form Aeolian-Skinner. Henry Clay Frick was a good customer, purchasing at least one other Aeolian for his New York City mansion, which now houses The Frick Collection. That organ is still heard regularly in recitals. The Princeton Aeolian was replaced during the 1960s with a neo-baroque organ built by the Gress-Miles Organ Co. Had it remained just a few more years, its aesthetic significance would have been recognised by the administration of the University and the concert-going public. Intact Aeolian organs, though not old by the standards of historic European instruments,

Alexander Russell, organist.

are already a great rarity.

In 1917, a new organ was installed in St. Paul's:

> St. Paul's Catholic Church has just received a gift of
> $5,000 for a new pipe organ, which is now under con-
> struction by the Haskell Company, Philadelphia . . .
> Twelve hundred and ten speaking pipes will be included
> in this new instrument. It will be a two-manual organ
> with an electric action. The outside pipes will be painted
> cream and gold to match the church decorations while
> the cabinet will be quartered oak.
>
> The new organ will be delivered in September and
> the instrument will be dedicated about the middle of that
> month. Several changes will be made in the choir loft and
> the gallery in connection with the installation of the in-
> strument.[21]

The inaugural program was held Thursday evening, 18 October 1917, but the local newspaper did not cover the recital.[22] This

---

21. "Organ Recital at St. Paul's," *The Princeton Packet*, 12 October 1917, p. 1.
22. *Ibid.*

John T. Austin, organbuilder.

Basil G. Austin, organbuilder.

The interior of the Austin Organ Co. (left). The Austin Organ Company about the time the company supplied an instrument to Trinity Church (above).

instrument survived until the present neo-Gothic church was built about 1955, when the organ was rebuilt by Chester A. Raymond of Princeton.

Trinity Church replaced its Odell organ of 1872 with a new instrument built by the Austin Organ Co., Opus 775 (1918). This firm was founded in 1899 by two brothers, John Turnell Austin (1869-1948) and Basil G. Austin (1874-1958), in Hartford, Connecticut, after beginning work in Detroit, Michigan. English-born, John and Basil were brilliant inventors and had about seventy patents to their credit. In January, 1937, the firm was reorganized as The Austin Organ Co., Inc., when it was run by Frederic B. Austin, and in 1973, Frederic's son, Donald Austin, became president. The firm is still active and respected today, nearly a century after its formation.

A notice in the *Princeton Packet* alerted townspeople of the impending inauguration:

ORGAN RECITAL AT TRINITY CHURCH By Sheldon B. Foote — Tuesday Evening at 8:30. The new organ just completed by the Austin Organ Company of Hartford, Conn., is to be formally opened Tuesday, Feb. 26, [1918] at 8:30 p.m. The recitalist will be Sheldon B.

Sheldon B. Foote, Princeton organist (above). Title page of an M. P. Möller catalogue, 1891 (right).

> Foote, Fellow of the American Guild of Organists and
> Master of the Choristers in Trinity Church . . .
> The organ is electrically controlled and modern in con-
> struction, the plan of the stops was drawn up by Mr.
> Foote and there are 74 stops and couplers on the console
> of which number 43 are speaking registers.[23]

Included in the program were the *Toccata and Fugue in D Minor* of
J.S. Bach, the *Fantasie Sonata* of Josef Rheinberger, and the *Fanfare* of
Jacques Lemmens. The organ served until it was replaced by the
Aeolian-Skinner Organ Co., with their Opus 1294 (1955), an organ
having three manuals with two swell divisions. Later, the church
acquired a Casavant Frères, Opus 3364 (1978), a four-manual
mechanical action instrument, which is still in use.

Other new organs followed. The organ in the Chapel of Princeton Theological Seminary was rebuilt by the Haskell firm in 1919.[24]
Little is known about this instrument: there was no coverage in the
local press, and the Haskell records seem not to have survived.

---

23. "Organ Recital at Trinity Church," *The Princeton Packet*, 1 March 1918, p. 6.
24. "Contracts Go To Haskell," *The Diapason* v. 10, no. 8 (1 July, 1919): 8.

ESTABLISHED 1880,

MÖLLER

CHURCH, CONCERT, CHAPEL, LODGE & CHAMBER

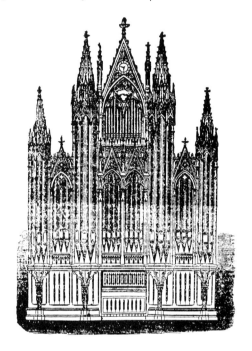

PIPE ORGANS,

M. P. MÖLLER, HAGERSTOWN, MD.

Specifications of One, Two, Three and Four Manual Organs furnished on application in Special catalogue, also, drawings prepared free of charge.

We do not print regular cuts or engravings of Pipe Organs. Every organ we build to suit the place and requirements.

We make special designs to harmonize with church furniture and the space the organ is to occupy.

77

During May, 1920, the erection of the Garden Theatre on Nassau Street was in progress by the Princeton Theatre Company. Every theatre of the time needed an organ, and on 23 April 1920, a contract was signed with M. P. Möller for a "Three-manual and pedal Duplex Concert Organ," the firm's Opus 2985. The price of the instrument was $7,000.[25]

The Möller company was established in 1875 by Mathias Peter Möller (1854-1937), a Danish immigrant, and in 1880 a factory was erected at Hagerstown, Maryland, where the firm continues to operate today under the leadership of Ronald R. Ellis. M.P. Möller is the single largest manufacturer of pipe organs in the history of organ-building, and by 1925, nearly 5,000 Möller organs had been built.

The delivery of the Princeton instrument was late. A letter from G. C. Wintringer, President of the Princeton Theatre Company, to Mr. Möller, recounts:

December 21, 1920.

Dear Sir,

Referring to your letter of the 9th, in reply to inquiry from our Mr. Walter H. Olden regarding the possible date of shipment of the organ for our theatre. We are sorry to learn that you may be unable to give us this organ by February 1st as previously promised. We trust you will do everything you possibly can to meet this date.

Our theatre was finished and opened for business the last week in September, so you can see that everything has been thoroughly dried out and there will be no condition of dampness to contend with as far as the organ is concerned . . . everything is in readiness for the organ.

Yours very truly,
G.C. Wintringer[26]

---

25. MS, Contract, M.P. Möller, Inc., Opus 2985, with the Princeton Theater Company, Princeton, New Jersey. Quoted with permission.
26. MS, Letter, G. C. Wintringer, President, Princeton Theatre Company to M. P. Möller, 21 December 1920. Quoted with permission.

Mathias P. Möller, organbuilder (above). The M. P. Möller factory (below).

The organ was shipped 20 February 1921, and arrived in Princeton 3 March. By early May the organ was completed, and a letter from Sheldon B. Foote relates:

May 17th 1921

Dear Mr. Möller:

It is with the greatest of pleasure that I write you concerning the organ recently placed in the Garden Theatre, Princeton. The Theatre is well adapted for the organ and in turn the organ is most responsive, the voicing [sic] of both flutes and reeds is admirable and in this connection I wish to express my appreciation of the good work done by Mr. Bean of Philadelphia whom you sent out to do the finishing work. We organists are naturally cranks, more or less, and his patience stood the test well . . .

Yours very cordially,
Sheldon B. Foote[27]

The Witherspoon Street Presbyterian Church followed the example of the Princeton Theatre Company, and also purchased a Möller organ, built as Opus 3274 (1922). The contract was signed 10 November 1921, and the organ was installed by Easter day, 1922; the cost was $2,500. It was a very small two-manual organ with most of the stops on the Great duplexed from the Swell. The instrument was sold by the local Möller representative, Louis Luberoff, who according to *The Diapason*, sold a record number of organs during 1920.[28]

The congregation was thrilled; a letter from the pastor, Augustus E. Bennett, states:

May Second 1922.

Dear Mr. Shulenberger:

Enclosed you will find a program of our opening exercises installing the organ. I wish to state that up to date the organ has met every expectation on our part and I

27. MS, Letter, Sheldon B. Foote, organist of Trinity Church, to Mr. M. P. Möller, 17 May 1921. Quoted with permission.
28. "Luberoff Has New Record," *The Diapason* v. 11, no. 3 (1 February 1920): 1.

know you would be pleased to hear the many com-
plimentary remarks made concerning the quality of
same. For myself, I can simply say that I am very pleased
with everything; moreover, I cannot express the gratifi-
cation I felt on Easter Sunday as I listened to the instrument and remembered how, according to promise, you
had so faithfully kept your word by placing the organ
within our Church, all set up and ready to be played
exactly when you stated, Easter Sunday. Believe me as I
tell you that I have not failed to tell any one that M.P.
Möller Pipe Organ Company can be depended upon to
deliver the goods when promised . . .

Most faithfully yours,
Augustus E. Bennett[29]

Despite its small dimensions, the organ served the church into the
1970s. Unfortunately, perhaps because the congregation of the
Witherspoon Street Presbyterian Church was black, there was no
account of the installation in the local newspaper.

Residence organs became increasingly common in the early
decades of the twentieth century, but only one is known to have been
installed in a Princeton residence before 1925. It was built by Reuben
Midmer & Son, during 1916.

The Midmer firm began in Brooklyn, New York, during 1860.
Reuben Midmer (1824-95), the founder, had worked during the
1850s for Richard M. Ferris (1818-58) and Levi U. Stuart (1827-
1904). Later, he was joined by his son, Reed Midmer, and in 1924,
the firm name was changed to Midmer-Losh, when Charles Seibert
Losh (1880-1934) became a partner.

Regarding the Princeton installation, *The Diapason* stated:

A divided electro-pneumatic organ is being completed
by Reuben Midmer & Son of Brooklyn in the residence,
Mercer Manor, of H.B. Owsley, Princeton, N.J.

---

29. MS, Letter, Pastor Augustus Eugene Bennett of Witherspoon Street Presbyterian Church, to E. O. Shulenberger, M.P. Möller, Co., Inc., 2 May 1922. Quoted
with permission.

Reuben Midmer, organbuilder.

Reed Midmer, organbuilder.

A self-player is attached to this instrument, which plays the melody on one manual and the accompaniment on the other. The case work of the organ is finished in white enamel with mahogany trim, while the detached console is in solid mahogany.[30]

The report included the stoplist, which is published in the appendix. The organ was eventually moved to another house, later placed in storage by incompetent persons, and sold in 1964 for $100.00. Portions of it exist in an amateur's installation in St. Luke's Episcopal Church, Charlestown, N.H.

By 1925, Princeton was firmly established as a center of education and affluence. This was due in part to the University, but also to its location half-way between the cities of New York and Philadelphia. Local church and collegiate institutions had the financial resources to replace old-fashioned instruments as musical tastes changed. Regrettably, not one Princeton organ built before 1925 survives in anything like its original condition.

---

30. "Organ in Residence is Made by Midmer," *The Diapason* v. 7, no. 10 (1 September 1916): 14.

Appendix:
Organ Contracts, Descriptions, and Stoplists.

The organ specifications presented herein were collected from a variety of sources. Some originated in published form, such as music journals or newspapers, while others survive only in manuscript. No attempt was made to force these stoplists into a standard format; rather, they are presented as found in their sources.

Trinity Church, Episcopal
Princeton, New Jersey
Hall & Labagh (1850)
Source: Hall & Labagh Correspondence, v. II, p. 13.

1. Open Diapason
2. Stop.^{d} Diapason Treble
3. Stop.^{d} Diapason Bass
4. Dulciano [*sic*]
5. Principal Treble
6. Principal Bass
7. Flute
8. Fifteenth
9. Trumpet
10. Pedal
11. Pedal Couple [*sic*]
12. Bellows

First Presbyterian Church
Princeton, New Jersey
George Jardine & Son (1864)
Relocated 1875 to
Witherspoon Street Presbyterian Church
Source: Notebook of Margaret Van Zandt Blackwell

GREAT ORGAN:
1. Open Diapason
2. Melodia
3. Stopped Diapason Bass
4. Viol di Gamba
5. Principal
6. Clariana
7. Twelfth
8. Fifteenth
9. Trumpet

SWELL ORGAN:
10. Open Diapason
11. Stopped Diapason
12. Dulciana
13. Violana
14. Flageolet
15. Hautboy
16. Tremulant

PEDAL ORGAN:
17. Bourdon

COUPLERS:
18. Great to Pedal
19. Swell to Pedal
20. Swell to Great

Old Chapel, College of New Jersey
Princeton, New Jersey
Hall & Labagh (1871)
Source: Reconstructed from F. R. Webber and Hall
correspondence by Stephen L. Pinel, 1987

GREAT ORGAN: 58 notes, [CC-a3]

Open Diapason	8'
Gamba	8'
Doppel Flute	8'
Stopped Diapason	8'
Principal	4'
Flute Harmonic	4'
Twelfth	2⅔'
Fifteenth	2'
Trumpet	8'
Swell to Great	
Swell to Great Octaves	

SWELL ORGAN: 58 notes, [CC-a3]

Bourdon Treble	16'
Bourdon Bass	16'
Open Diapason	8'
Viola d'Amour	8'
Stopped Diapason	8'
Principal	4'
Fifteenth	2'
Dolce Cornet	3 ranks
Cornopean	8'

PEDAL ORGAN: [27 notes, CCC-D?]

Open Diapason	16'
Bourdon	16'
Violoncello	8'
Great to Pedal	
Swell to Pedal	

Trinity Church, Episcopal
Princeton, New Jersey
J.H. & C.S. Odell, Opus 111 (1872)
Source: F. R. Webber Stoplist Collection

GREAT ORGAN: 58 notes, [CC-a3]

1	Open Diapason	8'	58
2	Keraulophon	8'	58
3	Dulce	8'	58
4	Clarionet Flute	8'	58
5	Principal	4'	58
6	Wald Flute	4'	46
7	Twelfth	2⅔'	58
8	Fifteenth	2'	58
9	Sesquialtera, 3 ranks		174
10	Trumpet	8'	58

SWELL ORGAN: 58 notes, [CC-a3]

11	Double Open Diapason	16'	46
12	Bourdon Bass	16'	12
13	Open Diapason	8'	58
14	Dulciana	8'	58
15	Stopped Diapason	8'	58
16	Violina	4'	58
17	Piccolo	2'	58
18	Oboe	8'	46
19	Bassoon	8'	12
20	Vox Humana (blank slide)		
	Tremulant		

PEDAL ORGAN: 27 notes, [CCC-D]
21 Grand Open Diapason   16' — 27

COUPLERS:
Swell to Great
Swell to Pedals
Great to Pedals
Patent reversible coupler
Bellows signal
Eight patent pneumatic compositions on Great

Alexander Hall, Princeton University
Princeton, New Jersey
George Jardine & Son (1896)
Source: *Musical Opinion and Music Trade Review*,
1 October 1896, p. 25.

GREAT: 61 notes, CC to C.

Open diapason	16'
Open diapason	8'
Dolcissimo	8'
Viola di gamba	8'
Melodia	8'
Octave	4'
Flute d'amour	4'
Octave quinte	2⅔'
Super octave	2'
Mixture	3 ranks
Trumpet	8'

SWELL: 61 notes, CC to C.

Bourdon (bass)	16'
Bourdon (treble)	16'
Violin diapason	8'
Salicional	8'
Aeoline	8'
Stopped diapason	8'
Voix céleste	8'
Flûte harmonique	4'
Violino	4'
Flautino	2'
Dolce cornet	3 ranks
Cornopean	8'
Oboe	8'

PEDAL: 30 notes, CC to F.

Open diapason	16'
Bourdon	16'
Flute	8'
Gedackt	8'
Quinte	10-2/3'

MECHANICAL REGISTERS:
Swell to great.
Great to pedal.
Swell to pedal.
Blower's signal.
Wind indicator.
Swell tremulant.

PEDAL MOVEMENTS:
Great forte.
Great mezzo.
Great piano.
Swell forte.
Swell mezzo.
Swell piano.
Balanced swell pedal.
Pneumatic action to manuals.
Tubular pneumatic action to pedal.

Marquand Chapel, Princeton University
Princeton, New Jersey
Müller & Abel (1897)

Source: *Princeton Press*, Saturday, 7 August 1897, p. 2.
[Exact quotation in full]

The instrument is a Two Manual and Pedal Organ of the larger type, located in two alcoves, on the right and left hand side of the pulpit, a distance of 45 feet between the two organs. It was built in New York City by Müller & Abel, 362 to 372 Second Ave. (late with the Roosevelt Organ Works.)

Reverting to the interior of the instrument, it can be said without qualification that the excellence, durability, and finish of the work in every detail however insignificant, have been carried to the highest attainable standard, that the instrument as a whole is a representative one of the perfection to which the art of organ building has been advanced, and that it is in every way worthy to stand in this superb chapel.

The organ contains 21 speaking stops (9 in the Great, 9 in the Swell and three in the Pedal Organ), it has 4 couplers, by which various parts of the organ can be combined, besides seven auxiliary pedal movements, including the Swell and the Crescendo and Diminuendo Pedal. The last named pedal is of a novel character and furnishes complete control over the entire instrument. By a single stroke on the former pedal, a gradual crescendo, or increase of tone, from the softest stop to the full organ, is obtained, without disturbing the existing arrangement of knobs, the rapidity of the crescendo being regulated by the degree of speed used in pressing down the pedal; a diminuendo, or reverse effect, is accomplished by raising up [*sic*] pedal slowly.

The Windchests are "tubular-pneumatic" in principle, and afford a separate pallet for every pipe. The construction and operation are such as to preclude the possibility of almost all of the derangements common to most organs, arising from thermometric or barometric variations. No matter how large the organ, these chests render the touch light and agreeable without the intervention of the complicated "pneumatic lever" and above all insure a degree of perfection in "repetition" never before attained in an organ, and equal to that of the most perfect pianoforte. They dispose with the objectionable sliders, heretofore commonly used, and are so arranged that each and every part is easy of access for removal or replacement in case of accident.

The blowing apparatus consists of a large bellows, with two square feeders, operated by a Ross piston water motor. From the bellows the compressed air is conveyed to a "regulator" to insure absolute steadiness, and from thence it is distributed to the different departments of the organ, each being supplied by a separate wind-trunk. Each trunk is fitted with a telescope joint to avoid the weight of windchests and pipes being transferred from the frame to it, by possible shrinkage, or the settling of the floor.

All the mechanism throughout the organ (though the amount has been greatly reduced by resorting to tubular pneumatic action for the key boards and drawstops) serves as a specially perfect sample of the highest class of workmanship. Although the distance between those two organs is forty-five feet, the longest tube about 55 feet, the repetition is instantaneous, something never attained in an organ before.

The voicing, on which mainly depends the success of the instrument is deserving of the close study and examination of those interested in the subject, combining all the best points of European schools with some effects seldom produced. The great delicacy and characteristic quality of tone in the different stops, the dignified power of full organ without harshness, and the perfect blending of the whole into an agreeable and massive tone, yet not lacking in brilliancy, are all noteworthy features and the result of a most careful and yet progressive instrument.

The specifications for the organ describe it as having two manuals, compass CC to C, 61 notes; and pedals CCC to F, 30 notes. Windchests, tubular pneumatic; combination action, fixed; key action, tubular, lead tubes throughout; blowing action, Ross water motor; wind pressure 3½ inch; pitch, international; material of case, quartered oak, richly carved; decoration of front pipes, oil color and gold.

No. of Stop: GREAT ORGAN.

1. Bourdon 16 ft. split knob 61 pipes.
2. Open Diapason 8 ft. 61 pipes.
3. Viola di Gamba 8 ft. 61 pipes.
4. Dulciana 8 ft. 61 pipes.
5. Doppelfloete 8 ft. 61 pipes.
6. Hohlfloete 4 ft. 61 pipes.
7. Octave 4 ft. 61 pipes.
8. Mixture (4 ranks) 12, 15, 17, 22; 244 pipes.
9. Trumpet 8 ft. 61 pipes.

SWELL ORGAN.

10. Open Diapason 8 ft. 61 pipes.
11. Spitzfloete 8 ft. 61 pipes.
12. Stopped Diapason 8 ft. 61 pipes.
13. Dolce 8 ft. 61 pipes.
14. Flute Harmonique 4 ft. 61 pipes.
15. Gemshorn 4 ft. 61 pipes.
16. Flageolet 2 ft. 61 pipes.
17. Cornopean 8 ft. 61 pipes.
18. Oboe 8 ft. 61 pipes.

PEDAL ORGAN.

19. Open Diapason 16 ft. 30 pipes.
20. Bourdon 16 ft. 30 pipes.
21. Violoncello 8 ft. 30 pipes.

COUPLERS.

22. Swell to Great.
23. Swell to Great Octaves.
24. Swell to Pedal.
25. Great to Pedal.

MECHANICAL REGISTERS.

26. Swell Tremulant.
27. Bellows Signal.
28. Dial Wind Indicator.

PEDAL MOVEMENTS.

29.–30. Two affecting Great and Pedal Stops.
31.–32. Two affecting Swell and Pedal Stops.
33. Full Organ Pedal (which also acts as
      Crescendo and Diminuendo Pedal).
34. Great to Pedal Reversing Pedal.
35. Balanced Swell Pedal.

SUMMARY.

Great Organ   9 stops — 732 pipes
Swell Organ   9 stops — 549 pipes
Pedal Organ   3 stops — 90 pipes
Total speaking stops: 21.
Total pipes: 1371.
Couplers 4.
Mechanical accessories 3.
Pedal Movements 7.
Total 35.

First Presbyterian Church
Princeton, New Jersey
Hillgreen, Lane & Co., Opus 28 (1902)
Source: *The Princeton Press,* Saturday, 3 May 1902, p. 4.
[Exact quotation in full]

FIRST CHURCH ORGAN

The First Presbyterian Church has just completed its new three-manual tubular pneumatic organ, given by Dr. and Mrs. William M. Paxton, as a memorial to their son, Harmar Denny Paxton, who died in 1896.

The organ was built by Hillgreen, Lane & Co., of Alliance, O., who have spared no pains to make it a perfect up-to-date instrument, with the latest mechanical devices and improvements.

The instrument has been passed by the experts employed by the trustees as perfect both in materials and workmanship.

The organ will be formally opened on Thursday evening, May 8th, at 8:15, with a recital in charge of Mr. Francis Cuyler van Dyck, who will be assisted by Mr. Edwin H. Kellogg, the organist of the church, and Mrs. Kuser, soprano, and Mr. Robert Hosea, the basso from the Fifth Avenue Presbyterian Church.

All the music lovers of Princeton are cordially invited to attend this recital.

The following is a description of the organ with specifications:

Perhaps no organ in the state is so liberally supplemented with mechanical devices for facilitating the work of the organist and augmenting the effectiveness of the instrument.

Chief among these is the extensive use of a coupler system by which the volume of tone obtainable is much more than double that of the mechanical organ of similar registration. Thus the playing of a simple chord on this instrument may produce simultaneous speech from more than six hundred pipes.

Then, too, the possibilities of tonal combinations are rendered well nigh inexhaustible.

Since the dynamic work of the action is effected pneumatically, the stress required of the finger for depressing a key is not increased by the addition of couplers. At all times, whether one stop or many be drawn, whether one or all the manuals be actuated, the "touch" remains the same.

Another unusual feature of the instrument is that beyond the compass of the 61 keys there are added 12 pipes to extend the effective range of the super-octave couplers throughout the entire key-scale. Thus the highest octave has also its complete super-duplicate.

Every desirable expedient known to scientific organ building has been employed in this instrument. Here are piston and pedal combinations, swell and choir balanced pedals, tilting tablets, coupler cancels, pneumatic key and draw-stop action and a crescendo device by which the registration is made to swell from the mere hint of sound in the Aeoline stop through all the range of tonal growth till the full organ's utmost power is reached.

For blowing the organ hydraulic power is furnished by two motors, located in the basement of the church, and operating two independent sets of bellows feeders.

Specifications of the Organ

Compass of manuals CC to C, 61 keys;
compass of pedals CCC to F, 30 keys.

GREAT ORGAN.

16-foot open diapason, metal, 73 pipes.
 8-foot open diapason, metal, 73 pipes.
 8-foot dulciana, metal, 73 pipes.
 8-foot gamba, metal, 73 pipes.
 8-foot doppel floete, wood, 73 pipes.
 4-foot principal, metal, 73 pipes.
 4-foot rohr flute, wood, 73 pipes.
 2-foot super octave, metal, 61 pipes.
 3, 4 and 5 rnk. mixture, metal, 245 pipes.
 8-foot trumpet, metal, 61 pipes.

SWELL ORGAN.

16-foot bourdon, wood, 73 pipes.

8-foot open diapason, metal, 73 pipes.

8-foot salicional, metal, 73 pipes.

8-foot stopped diapason, wood, 73 pipes.

8-foot aeoline, metal, 73 pipes.

8-foot vox celeste (augm't'd), metal, 73 pipes.

4-foot gemshorn, metal, 73 pipes,

4-foot flute harmonic, wood and metal, 73 pipes.

2-foot flautina, metal, 61 pipes.

3-rnk. dolce cornet, metal, 183 pipes.

8-foot oboe and bassoon, metal, 61 pipes.

8-foot vox humana or coropean [*sic*], metal, 61 pipes.

swell tremulant.

CHOIR ORGAN.

8-foot geigen principal, metal, 73 pipes.

8-foot dolce, metal, 73 pipes.

8-foot concert flute, wood, 73 pipes.

4-foot flute d'amour, wood and metal, 73 pipes.

2-foot piccolo, metal, 61 pipes.

8-foot clarinet, metal, 61 pipes.

choir tremulant.

PEDAL ORGAN.

16-foot open diapason, wood, 30 keys, 42 pipes.

16-foot bourdon, wood, 30 keys, 42 pipes.

16-foot lieblich gedacht (borrowed from II), 30 keys, 42 pipes.

8-foot violoncello, metal, 30 keys, 42 pipes.

COUPLERS.

Swell to great.

great to pedal.

swell to pedal.

choir to pedal.

swell suboctave to great.
swell superoctave to great.
choir to great.
choir suboctave to great.
great superoctave to great.
great suboctave to great.
swell to choir.
swell superoctave to choir.
swell superoctave to swell.
pedal to pedal octave.
choir superoctave to choir.

PISTON COMBINATIONS.
Each drawing an appropriate pedal support.
Great organ full.
great organ mezzo.
great organ pianissimo.
choir organ full.
choir organ mezzo.
choir organ piano.
swell organ full.
swell organ mezzo.
swell organ pianissimo.

ACCESSORIES.
Great coupler cancel.
swell coupler cancel.
choir coupler cancel.
wind indicator.
crescendo dial.
motor starter.

PEDAL MOVEMENTS.

Great organ full.

great organ piano.

choir organ piano.

swell organ full.

swell organ piano.

great to pedal reversible.

balanced swell pedal.

balanced choir pedal.

full organ.

crescendo and diminuendo pedal.

Second Presbyterian Church
Princeton, New Jersey
H. Hall & Co. (1912)

Source: *The Diapason* v. 3, no. 3, 1 February 1912, p. 1.

GREAT ORGAN.

16 ft. Bourdon, 61 pipes.

8 ft. First Open Diapason, 61 pipes.

8 ft. Second Open Diapason, 61 pipes.

8 ft. Gamba, 61 pipes.

8 ft. Spitz Flute, 61 pipes.

8 ft. Dulciana, 61 pipes.

8 ft. Doppel Flute, 61 pipes.

4 ft. Octave, 61 pipes.

4 ft. Flute d'Amour, 61 pipes.

8 ft. Tuba (on heavy wind), 61 pipes.

SWELL ORGAN.

16 ft. Lieblich Gedacht, 73 pipes.

8 ft. Open Diapason, 73 pipes.

8 ft. Salicional, 73 pipes.

8 ft. Viole d'Orchestre, 73 pipes.

8 ft. Viole Celeste, 61 pipes.

8 ft. Stopped Diapason, 73 pipes.

8 ft. Aeoline, 73 pipes.

4 ft. Flute Harmonic, 73 pipes.

3 rk. Dolce Cornet, 183 pipes.

2 ft. Flautino, 61 pipes.

8 ft. Cornopean, 73 pipes.

8 ft. Oboe, 73 pipes.

PEDAL ORGAN.

16 ft. Open Diapason, 32 notes.

16 ft. Dulciana, 32 notes.

16 ft. Bourdon, 32 notes.

16 ft. Lieblich Gedacht, 32 notes.

16 ft. Violone, 32 notes.

8 ft. Flute, 32 notes.

8 ft. Violoncello, 32 notes.

COUPLERS — Swell to great unison. Swell to great sub. Swell to great super. Great to great super. Swell sub. Swell super. Swell unison off. Swell to pedal. Great to pedal.

COMBINATIONS — Five pistons operating great organ stops. Six pistons operating swell organ stops. Three pistons operating pedal organ stops.

ACCESSORIES — Balanced swell pedal. Balanced crescendo pedal. Full organ pedal. Swell tremolo. Wind indicator. Crescendo indicator.

[The Pedal division probably had 4 ranks of 32 pipes each, two of which were extended to 8' stops, with 12 additional pipes each.]

Procter Hall, Graduate College
Princeton, New Jersey
Aeolian Company, Opus 1334 (1916)
Source: Contract, 26 June 1915
[Exact quotation in full]

The Aeolian Company / Pipe-Organ Department / Aeolian Hall
New York. John W. Keins, Managing director; Frank Taft, Art
Director / Builders of Aeolian-Pipe-Organs for Residences / 29 West
Forty-Second Street. June 16, 1915. Specification for an Aeolian
Pipe-Organ prepared for Procter Hall, Princeton University,
Princeton, New Jersey.

Four Manuals, Compass CC to c4; and Pedals, Compass CCC to
F. (All speaking stops not otherwise indicated are of 8 ft. pitch)

MANUAL I (Great)
1. Diapason F
2. Diapason (high) 4'
3. Diapason 2'
4. Diapason (Mixture)
5. String F
6. String MF
7. Flute F
8. Flute P
9. Flute (high) 4'
10. Trumpet (deep) 16'
11. Trumpet

MANUAL II (Swell)
(All stops practical to include 73 pipes)
12. Diapason F (English)
13. String F ⎫ Same scale etc., and full
14. String F (Vibrato) ⎬ compass of pipes.
15. String MF ⎫ Ditto.
16. String MF (Vibrato) ⎬

17. String P
18. String P (Vibrato)
19. String (Dolce Cornet)
20. Flute (deep) 16'
21. Flute P
22. Flute (high) 4'
23. Flageolet 2'
24. Bassoon (deep) 16'
25. Trumpet
26. Oboe
27. Vox Humana

} Ditto.

MANUAL III (Choir) – 3 1/2 inch wind pressure.
28. Diapason F (Geigen Principal)
29. String (deep) 16'
30. String MF
31. String MF Vibrato
32. Flute F
33. Flute P
34. Flute (Quintadena)
35. Flute (high) 4'
36. Piccolo 2'
37. Clarinet
38. Oboe (Orchestral)

} Same scale etc. and full compass full toned rich Viol d'Orchestre pipes.

MANUAL IV (Antiphonal Organ)
(All stops to include 73 pipes if possible)
39. Diapason
40. Flute (Clarabella or Melodia)
41. Flute (Old style Stopped Diapason)
42. Flute (high) 4'
43. Flute (deep) 16'
44. String MF
45. String MF (Vibrato)
46. String P (Dolce Cornet)

} same scale etc. and full compass of pipes.

47. String PP (Aeoline)
48. String (high) 4' (Violino)
49. Vox Humana

PEDAL ORGAN (30 notes)
(Pedal-board to be straight and concave. Long keys.)
50. Diapason (deep) 16'
51. String F (deep) 16'
52. String P (deep) 16' (from No. 29.)
53. String F 8'
54. Flute F (deep) 16'
55. Flute F (deep) 16' – from No. 20.
56. Flute 8'
57. Trumpet F (deep) 16'
58. Bassoon P (deep) 16' – from No. 24.
59. Flute (deep) 16'F   } Located with
60. Flute (deep) P – from No. 43 } Antiphonal Organ

PERCUSSION INSTRUMENTS
61. Harp (Augmented) 61 notes.
    (Played from Manuals I, III, and IV)
62. Chimes 20 notes.
    (Played from Manuals I, III, and IV)

COUPLERS
(Affecting only Octave and Sub Octave Couplers specified)
63. Swell to Great
64. Swell to Great Octave
65. Swell to Great Sub
66. Choir to Swell
67. Choir to Swell Octave
68. Choir to Swell Sub
69. Swell Octave
70. Swell Sub
7i Great Octave

72. Great Sub
73. Choir to Great
74. Choir to Great Sub
75. Choir Octave
76. Choir Sub
77. Antiphonal to Great
78. Antiphonal to Great Octave
79. Antiphonal to Swell
80. Antiphonal to Choir
81. Antiphonal Octave
82. Antiphonal Sub
83. Great to Pedal
84. Swell to Pedal
85. Swell to Pedal Octave
86. Choir to Pedal
87. Antiphonal to Pedal

ADJUSTABLE COMBINATION PISTONS
(Located under Swell Organ Manual)

88-94. Six Adjustable Tutti Combinations and Release, affective on entire organ including Antiphonal, Harp, and Chimes. (To be spaced between sharp keys.)

95. Stop-Action Connection
96. Stop-Action Release

With these pistons, located at left side of Comb. Pistons, the tablet Stop-Action can be made active or inactive as desired.

97. Coupler Combination
(Two Pistons or one tablet to be determined.)

ACCESSORIES
98. Sforzando
99. Tonal (Acting on all stops except Antiphonal)
100. Antiphonal Tonal
101. Great & Choir Expression
102. Swell Expression

103. Antiphonal Expression
104. Tutti Expression (General-Swell for entire Main Organ)
105. Antiphonal Only (Silencing all Main Organ stops and couplers)
106. Great Silent
107. Swell Silent
108. Choir Silent ⎫ Draw-Stops.
109. Antiphonal Silent (Pedal & Manual) ⎬
110. Pedal Silent ⎭
111. Great to Pedal Reversible
112. Swell to Pedal Reversible
113. Choir to Pedal Reversible
114. Antiphonal to Pedal Reversible
115. Great Tremolo ⎫ Tablets located with their
116. Swell Tremolo ⎬ respective departments; no
117. Choir Tremolo ⎪ Tremolo to act below
118. Antiphonal Tremolo ⎭ Tenor "C."

AEOLIAN SOLO MUSIC ROLL CONTROLS

119. Normal, Reverse and Unison Lever
   (Acting only on Swell, Great and Pedal)
120. Choir Upper Holes
121. Choir Lower Holes
122. Antiphonal Upper Holes
123. Antiphonal Lower Holes
124. Aeolian Tempo
125. Aeolian Reroll
126. Aeolian Ventil

GENERAL DETAILS.

(a) LOCATION: Organ to be located in Gallery. Antiphonal Organ to be located in basement under bay window, floor of which is to be provided with an opening for tone exit.

(b) CONSOLE: Console containing keyboards as well as Aeolian Solo Music Roll mechanism to be detached and located in Gallery at side of Organ. Manual keys to be of long type, and backs of sharps bevelled.

(c) BLOWING APPARATUS: Blowing apparatus to be located in basement. Electric motors, generators, and starting switch to be provided by Organ builders; one generator for keyboards, draw-stop action, and swell engines, and another generator for fresh wind boxes only.

(d) CASEWORK, ETC. Casework for Organ and Console, re-inforcing Gallery floor, preparation for Antiphonal grille, are included in this contract, and all of this work is to be done under the direction and supervision of the Architects, Cram & Ferguson.

CONTRACT

We hereby agree to build an Aeolian Pipe-Organ in accordance with the foregoing Specification and General Details, which are hereby made a part of this contract, of the highest attainable standard of quality in both workmanship and materials throughout, for Mr. H. C. Frick, and to deliver and install same in Procter Hall, Princeton University, New Jersey, ready for use not later than May 1st, 1916, for and in consideration of the sum Forty-six Thousand Dollars, ($46,000.00), Eight Thousand, Two Hundred and Sixty-eight Dollars and Fifty cents, ($8,268.50), to be paid as Messrs. Cram & Ferguson render their bills to us, and the balance, Thirty-seven Thousand, Seven Hundred and Thirty-one Dollars, and Fifty cents, ($37,731.50), to be paid in cash on satisfactory completion of the Organ.

Organ to be at risk of The Aeolian Company until accepted.

THE AEOLIAN COMPANY, [signed, *Frank Taft*] Pipe-Organ Department. ACCEPTED BY: [signed, *H. C. Frick*], This 6th day of July, 1915.

H. B. Owlsey Residence
Princeton, New Jersey
Reuben Midmer & Son (1916)

Source: *The Diapason* v. 7, no. 10, 1 September 1916, p. 14.

GREAT ORGAN.
1. Open Diapason, 8 ft.
2. Viola di Gamba, 8 ft.
3. Dolce, 8 ft.
4. Concert flute, 8 ft.
5. Flute d'Amour, 4 ft.
   All of great in box, except open diapason.

SWELL ORGAN.
6. Bourdon, 16 ft.
7. Violin Diapason, 8 ft.
8. Salicional, 8 ft.
9. Vox Celeste, 8 ft.
10. Lieblich Gedeckt, 8 ft.
11. Violina, 4 ft.
12. Oboe, 8 ft.
13. Vox Humana (in separate box), 8 ft.

PEDAL ORGAN:
14. Sub Bass, 16 ft.
15. Lieblich Gedeckt, 16 ft.
16. Flute, 8 ft.
    There are seven piston combinations.
    An electric blower supplies the wind.

Trinity Church, Episcopal
Princeton, New Jersey
Austin Organ Co., Opus 775 (1918)
Source: Original Contract

GREAT ORGAN.

Double Open Diapason	16'	61 pipes
First Open Diapason	8'	61 "
Second Open Diapason	8'	61 "
Gross Flute	8'	61 "
Gamba (X)	8'	61 "
Claribel Flute (X)	8'	61 "
Gemshorn (X)	8'	61 "
Wald Flute (X)	4'	61 "
Octave	4'	61 "
Fifteenth	2'	61 "
Tuba (X)	8'	61 "

Great 16'
Great 8' (Unison Off)
Great 4'
Swell to Great 16'
Swell to Great 8'
Swell to Great 4'
Choir to Great 16'
Choir to Great 8'
Choir to Great 4'

Eight adjustable combination pistons to control Great stops.
(X) Enclosed in Choir Box

SWELL ORGAN.

Bourdon	16'	73 pipes
Diapason Phonon	8'	73 "
Horn Diapason	8'	73 "
Rohr Flute	8'	73 "

Viole d'Orchestre	8'	73	"
Viole Celeste	8'	73	"
Aeoline	8'	73	"
Flauto Traverso	4'	73	"
Violina	4'	73	"
Piccolo	2'	61	"
Mixture	3 Ranks	183	"
Double Oboe Horn	16'		
Oboe	8'	85	"
Clarion	4'		
Vox Humana	8'	61	"
Cornopean	8'	73	"
Tremolo			

Swell 16'
Swell 8' (Unison Off)
Swell 4'

Eight adjustable combination pistons to control Swell stops.

CHOIR ORGAN.

Contra Gamba	16'	73	"
Open Diapason	8'	73	"
Concert Flute	8'	73	"
Unda Maris	8'	73	"
Keraulophon	8'	73	"
Dulciana	8	73	"
Flute d'Amour	4'	73	"
Clarinet	8'	73	"
Orchestral Oboe	8'	73	"
Tremolo			
Gross Flute (From Great)	8'	61 notes	
Tuba (From Great)	8'	61	"

Choir 16'
Choir 8' (Unison Off)
Choir 4'
Swell to Choir 16'

Swell to Choir 8'
Swell to Choir 4'
Eight adjustable combination pistons to control Choir stops.

PEDAL ORGAN.

Resultant Bass	32'	32 notes
Open Diapason	16'	44 pipes
Second Open Diapason		
(From Great)	16'	32 notes
Bourdon	16'	44 pipes
Lieblich Gedeckt		
(From Swell)	16'	32 notes
Gamba (From Choir)	16'	32 "
Gedeckt (From Bdn.)	8'	32 "
Octave (From Open)	8'	32 "
Cello (From Gamba)	8'	32 "
Double Oboe Horn		
(From Swell)	16'	32 "
Trombone (Tuba		
Extension 12 pipes)	16'	32 "

Swell to Pedal 8'
Swell to Pedal 4'
Great to Pedal 8'
Choir to Pedal 8'

Six adjustable combination pedals to control Pedal stops.
Eight extra adjustable combination pistons placed over upper manual controlling entire organ, including couplers.

ACCESSORY.

Balanced Crescendo Pedal, adjustable, not moving registers
Balanced Swell Pedal
Balanced Choir & Great Pedal
Great to Pedal, Reversible
Sforzando Pedal

Princeton Theatre
Princeton, New Jersey.
M. P. Möller, Opus 2985 (1921)
Source: Möller Archives.

No. 2985 / Contract and Specifications / of / THREE MAN-UAL PIPE ORGAN / For / Princeton Theatre, / Princeton, N.J. / To Be Completed / Jan'y 23rd / 1921 / Price, $7,000.00 / From / M.P. MÖLLER, Pipe Organ Builder / HAGERSTOWN, MD. / U.S.A.

MEMORANDUM of AGREEMENT, Made this twenty-third day of April A.D., 1920, by and between M.P. Möller, of Hagerstown, Maryland, party of the first part, and the Princeton Theatre Co., party of the second part.

WITNESSETH: – That the party of the first part hereby agrees to build an organ after and according to the annexed specifications and plans to be hereafter approved by party of second part, and to erect it in the Princeton Theatre, Princeton, N.J. ready for use on or before the 23rd day of January A.D., 1921 or as soon thereafter as possible in the event of delays beyond his control.

2. The party of the first part agrees that the organ when completed shall be first class, free from defects in material or workmanship, and that the party of the second part may have the organ examined immediately on completion, by a competent and disinterested expert, and if said examination shows that the organ does not conform with this agreement the party of the first part agrees to remedy said defects at his own expense.

3. The party of the first part guarantees the action and construction of the organ for a term of five years from the date of completion and agrees to correct defects in material or workmanship that may be brought to his attention within that time, without cost to the party of the second part. This does not include tuning or ordinary care of the organ (or electric motors which are guaranteed by the manufacturers for one year).

4. In consideration of the above, the party of the second part agrees to pay M.P. Möller, or his order, the sum of Seven Thousand Dollars ($ 7000.00) AS FOLLOWS: Seven Hundred Dollars ($700.00)

on execution of the contract, and Six Thousand Three Hundred Dollars ($6,300.00) on completion of the work.

5. The party of the second part also agrees that the building will be in proper condition for the installation of the organ four (4) weeks previous to date of completion; that they will allow, free of interruption, suitable convenience and opportunity for the installation in the building, provide such a condition of quiet as is necessary for the proper tone regulation and tuning of the instrument, and necessary light, heat and power.

6. The party of the second part also agrees to insure the organ or its parts against loss by fire, water, etc., as soon as the parts are placed in the building, for the benefit of the parties hereto, as their interests may appear.

7. When water or electric motor is included in specifications, party of the second part agrees to provide foundation and enclosures when necessary; to furnish and install wind conductor between blower and organ; to do all wiring or plumbing connected therewith; to install such lights as may beneeded for the erection and future care of the organ, and do any necessary cutting of floors, partitions, or other parts of the building. In the event that local regulations require the use of an automatic remote control motor starter, electrical conduits or other special equipment they are to be furnished by party of the second part.

8. It is mutually understood that the title and ownership of the organ shall remain with party of the first part until the contract price, before mentioned, has been fully paid, after which the instrument shall become the property of the party of the second part; also that all verbal agreements and understandings are merged in this contract, and the specifications and details of construction attached hereto.

IN WITNESS WHEREOF we have hereunto set our hands and seals this day and year first above written.

M. P. Möller   Princeton Theatre Co.
by C W [illeg.]   G.C. Wintringer, Pres.
Party of the first part   Sheldon B. Foote
      Party of the second part

SPECIFICATIONS
of
THREE MANUAL DUPLEX CONCERT ORGAN

MANUALS: — Compass CC to c4, 61 Notes.
PEDALS: — Compass CCC to G, 32 Notes.
ACTION: — Möller's Electro-pneumatic throughout
STOPS: — Controlled by colored keys
Two Swell Boxes

GREAT ORGAN

1	8'	Open Diapason	85 Pipes
2	8'	Violin D'Orchestra, from #11	73 Notes
3	8'	Doppel Flute	73 Pipes
4	4'	Octave, from #1	73 Notes
5	4'	Zart Flute, from #10	61 "
6	2'	Piccolo, from #13	61 "
7	3	Rks Mixture, from #10-12-13	61 "
8	16'	Bass Clarinet, Tenor C, from #16	61 "
8a		Chimes	30 Notes

ORCHESTRAL ORGAN

9	8'	Horn Diapason (Synthethic)	73 Notes
10	8'	Quintadena	73 Pipes
11	8'	Violin D'Orchestra	73 Pipes
12	8'	Viola Celeste, Tenor C	73 "
13	4'	Flute Harmonic (Ex. Large & Brilliant)	73 "
14	8'	Orchestral Oboe	73 "
15	16'	Fagotto, Tenor C, from #14	61 Notes
16	8'	Clarinet	73 Pipes
16a		Concert Harp	37 Notes
		Tremulant	

SOLO ORGAN

17	8'	Gross Flute (Big)	85 Pipes
18	8'	Concert Flute	73 "
19	8'	Violin Cello	73 "
20	4'	Flute Overte - Tenor G, from #17	53 Notes
21	8'	Tuba	73 Pipes

22	16'	Bass Tuba — Tenor C, from #21	61 Notes
23	8'	Vox Humana	73 Pipes

PEDAL ORGAN

24	16'	Sub Bass — from #17	32 Notes
25	16'	Lieblich Gedeckt — from #24	32 "
26	8'	Violon Cello — from #19	32 "
27	8'	Flute — from #18	32 "

COUPLERS

28	Solo to Great	36	Orchestral to Solo
29	Solo to Great 4'	37	Solo 4'
30	Solo to Great 16'	38	Solo 16'
31	Orchestral to Great	39	Orchestral 4'
32	Orchestral to Great 4'	40	Orchestral 16'
33	Orchestral to Great 16'	41	Solo to Pedal
34	Great 4'	42	Orchestral to Pedal
35	Solo to Orchestral	43	Great to Pedal
		44	Great to Pedal 4'

MECHANICALS

45	Orchestral Tremulant	47	Echo Tremulant
46	Solo Tremulant	48	Crescendo Indicator

ADJUSTABLE COMBINATIONS
(Operated by Pistons placed under respective manuals.)

Piston No. 1
Piston No. 2
Piston No. 3
Piston No. 4   } Affecting Orchestral and Pedal
Piston No. 5
Piston No. 6

Piston No. 1
Piston No. 2
Piston No. 3
Piston No. 4   } Affecting Great and Pedal
Piston No. 5
Piston No. 6

Piston No. 1
Piston No. 2
Piston No. 3   } Affecting Solo and Pedal
Piston No. 4
Piston Couplers.
Corresponding Orchestral and Solo Pistons to Great Pistons.
Corresponding Pedal Pistons to Manual Pistons.

PEDAL MOVEMENTS

1   Great to Pedal Reversible.
2   Balanced Solo Pedal.
3   Balanced Orchestral Pedal.
4   Orchestral to Pedal Reversible.
5   Grand Crescendo Pedal.
Organ Bench with Music Shelf.
Concave Pedal.
Electric Blower and Generator of ample capacity.

April 20th, 1920
Cameron.

Witherspoon Street Presbyterian Church
Princeton, New Jersey.
M. P. Möller, Opus 3274 (1922)
Source: Möller Archives.

No. 3274 / CONTRACT and SPECIFICATIONS / of / 2 MANUAL PIPE ORGAN / For / Witherspoon St Presby Ch / Princeton, N.J. / TO BE COMPLETED / EASTER, 1922 / Price, $2500.00 / From / M.P. MÖLLER, Pipe Organ Builder / HAGERSTOWN, MD. / U.S.A.

MEMORANDUM of AGREEMENT, Made this 10th day of November, A.D., 1921, by and between M.P. Möller, of Hagerstown, Maryland, party of the first part, and Witherspoon St. Presbyterian Church, Princeton, N.J., party of the second part.

WITNESSETH: — That the party of the first part hereby agrees to build an organ after and according to the annexed specifications and plans to be hereafter approved by party of second part, and to erect it in above church ready for use on or before the Easter day of A.D., 1922, or as soon thereafter as possible in the event of delays beyond his control.

2. The party of the first part agrees that the organ when completed shall be first class, free from defects in material or workmanship, and that the party of the second part may have the organ examined immediately on completion, by a competent and disinterested expert, and if said examination shows that the organ does not conform with this agreement the party of the first part agrees to remedy said defects at his own expense.

3. The party of the first part guarantees the action and construction of the organ for a term of five years from the date of completion and agrees to correct defects in material or workmanship that may be brought to his attention within that time, without cost to the party of the second part. This does not include tuning or ordinary care of the organ (or electric motors which are guaranteed by the manufacturers for one year).

4. In consideration of the above, the party of the second part

agrees to pay M. P. Möller, or his order, the sum of Twenty- five hundred Dollars ($2500.00), AS FOLLOWS: 1/3 cash on completion, balances payable in one or two equal annual notes bearing 6% interest.

5. The party of the second part also agrees that the building will be in proper condition for the installation of the organ two weeks previous to the date of completion; that they will allow, free from interruption, suitable convenience and opportunity for the installation in the building, provide such a condition of quiet as is necessary for the proper tone regulation and tuning of this instrument, and necessary light, heat and power.

6. The party of the second part also agrees to insure the organ or its parts against loss by fire, water, etc., as soon as the parts are placed in the building, for the benefit of the parties hereto, as their interests may appear.

7. When water or electric motor is included in specifications, party of the second part agrees to provide foundation and enclosures when necessary; to provide and install wind conductor between blower and organ; to do all wiring or plumbing connected therewith; to install such lights as may be needed for the erection and future care of the organ, and to do any necessary cutting of floors, partitions, or other parts of the building. In the event that local regulations require the use of an automatic remote control motor starter, electrical conduits of other special equipments they are to be furnished by party of second part.

8. It is mutually agreed that the title and ownership of the organ shall remain with the party of the first part until the contract price, before mentioned, has been fully paid, after which the instrument shall become the property of the party of the second part; also that all verbal agreements and understandings are merged in this contract, and the specifications and details of construction attached hereto.

IN WITNESS WHEREOF we have hereunto set our hands and seals this day and year first mentioned above written.

WITNESS   M.P. Möller, Inc.
                              Witherspoon St. Presbyterian Church
                                     per H.B. Wexwood, Tres.
                                     Fred Vanzant, Luis Tillman

_____

SPECIFICATIONS
OF TWO MANUAL PIPE ORGAN

MANUALS: — Compass CC to C, 61 Notes.
PEDALS: — Compass CCC to G, 32 Notes.
ACTION: — Möller's Patent Tubular-Pneumatic throughout.
Stops controlled by Stop Keys.
Casting to be made of oak.
Pipes to be decorated in gold bronze.
Duplex Chest.

GREAT ORGAN

1	8'	Open Diapason	61 Pipes
2	8'	Stopped Diapason	61 "
3	8'	Dulciana. 12 from #2	61 "
4	8'	Flute Traverso	61 "

SWELL ORGAN

5	8'	Gedackt	61 Notes
6	4'	Flute	61 "
7	8'	Dolce	61 "
8	8'	Vox Celeste	49 Pipes

PEDAL ORGAN

9	16'	Bourdon	32 Pipes

COUPLERS

10   Great to Pedal
11   Swell to Pedal
12   Swell to Great
13   Swell to Great 16'
14   Swell to Great 4'
15   Swell 4'
16   Great 4'

MECHANICALS

17 Tremulant
    Crescendo Indicator

ADJUSTABLE COMBINATIONS
(Operated by pistons placed under respective manuals)
Piston No. 1
Piston No. 2   Affecting Great and Pedal Stops
Piston No. 1
Piston No. 2   Affecting Swell and Pedal Stops

PEDAL MOVEMENTS
1 Great to Pedal Reversible
2 Balanced Swell Pedal
3 Grand Crescendo Pedal

Organ Bench with Music Shelf of same material as Casting. /
Concave Pedal / Electric Blower of ample capacity.

Luberoff.
3/10/21.

Additions, Corrections, and Notes.

A frequent error by current historians is the failure to record events as they occur. The following three pages are included to record additions, corrections, and current information. Just as *Old Organs of Princeton* was going to press, a copy of the dedication program for the monumental E. M. Skinner organ, Opus 656 (1927), built for the University Chapel, surfaced.

Additions, Corrections, and Notes.

Additions, Corrections, and Notes.

Informal Recital

and

Demonstration

of

The Memorial Organ

in

The University Chapel

ARRANGED BY THE SKINNER ORGAN COM-
PANY, BUILDERS OF THE CHAPEL ORGAN,
IN CONJUNCTION WITH THE N. A. O., AND
PRESENTED WITH THE KIND CO-OPERATION
OF PRINCETON UNIVERSITY

SATURDAY AFTERNOON

October 13, 1928
at four o'clock

Princeton, New Jersey

PROGRAMME

A WORD OF WELCOME

BY

ALEXANDER RUSSELL

University Director of Music

I

(*a*)   Fantasie Dialogue   *Boellmann*
(*b*)   Pantomime   *Jepson*

     Played by CHANDLER GOLDTHWAITE.

II

(*a*)   Passacaglia and Fugue in C Minor   *Bach*
(*b*)   Choral No. 3 in A Minor   *Franck*

     Played by CHARLES M. COURBOIN. *Formerly Organist of Antwerp Cathedral. Now Soloist, Grand Court Organ, Philadelphia.*

III

(*a*)   Marche Pontificale (First Symphony)   *Widor*
(*b*)   Reverie on the Hymn Tune "University"   *Grace*

     Played by LYNNWOOD FARNAM. *Organist, Church of The Holy Communion, New York. Head of Organ Department, Curtis Institute, Philadelphia.*

IV

Improvisation on themes to be presented

     Played by ROLLO MAITLAND. *Organist of The Church of The New Jerusalem, Philadelphia.*

V

Allegro e Fuga "Ad Nos"   *Liszt*

     Played by FERNANDO GERMANI. *Organist of The Augusteo, Rome, Italy.*

VI

Choral No. 1 in E Major   *Franck*

     Played by RALPH W. DOWNES. *Choirmaster and Director of Music in The Princeton Chapel.*

THE ORGAN

T HE ORGAN is a memorial instrument, the gift of the donor who desires to remain anonymous for the present.

It was constructed by the Skinner Organ Company of Boston. In the preparation of the specifications, Dr. Alexander Russell, University Director of Music, had the co-operation of Charles M. Courboin, the eminent Belgian organist and organ architect (formerly of Antwerp Cathedral); Marcel Dupré, the noted French organist, formerly of Notre Dame Cathedral, Paris; Henry M. Willis, of London, and Ernest M. Skinner and Donald Harrison, of the Skinner Organ Company.

The instrument consists of five divisions played from a console of four manuals and pedals. The south chamber contains the Great, Swell, Choir, and Pedal organs; the north chamber, the Solo Organ. With the exception of the Great and Pedal Divisions, the different sections are enclosed in expression boxes. Two blowers (of 10 and 15 horse-power), located in the crypt, furnish wind, one being used for the low pressure, the other for the high pressure. The wind pressures vary from six to twenty-five inches. There are ninety-eight registers operating eighty-six "speaking stops," and nearly 6,000 pipes. The Pedal Division includes three "stops" of 32-ft. pitch. Every modern mechanical improvement of legitimate usefulness has been included in the specification. Provision has been made for the addition of an antiphonal organ in the west end of the Chapel (in the triforium) should this be found desirable at some future time.

The richly carved organ cases are also the gift of the same anonymous donor. In the medallions of the cases are personifications of the eight tones of Gregorian Music.

GREAT ORGAN (unenclosed)

	PIPES
32 ft. Quintaton	49
16 ft. Diapason	61
16 ft. Bourdon (Pedal Extension)	17
8 ft. First Diapason	61
8 ft. Second Diapason	61
8 ft. Third Diapason	61
8 ft. Principal Flute	61
8 ft. Doppel Flute*	61
5 1/3 ft. Quint	61
4 ft. Octave	61
4 ft. Principal	61
4 ft. Flute*	61
3 1/5 ft. Tenth	61
2 2/3 ft. Twelfth	61
2 ft. Fifteenth	61
Harmonics (V Ranks)	
15, 17, 19, 21, 22	305
Plein Jeu (III to VI Ranks)	268
16 ft. Contra Tromba*	61
8 ft. Tromba*	61
4 ft. Octave Tromba*	61

* Enclosed in Choir Box

SWELL ORGAN

	PIPES
16 ft. Bourdon	73
8 ft. Diapason	73
8 ft. Geigen Diapason	73
8 ft. Rohrflœte	73
8 ft. Flute Celeste	61
8 ft. Flauto Dolce	73
8 ft. Gamba	73
8 ft. Gamba Celeste	73
8 ft. Salicional	73
8 ft. Voix Celeste	73
4 ft. Octave	73
4 ft. Flute Triangulaire	73
2 ft. Piccolo	61
Chorus Mixture (V Ranks)	305
8 ft. Cor de Nuit	
4 ft. Fugara	
2 2/3 ft. Nazard	Cornet (V Ranks) . 305
2 ft. Flautino	drawing
1 3/5 ft. Tierce	separately
16 ft. Posaune	73
8 ft. Cornopean	73
8 ft. French Trumpet	73
8 ft. Oboe	73
8 ft. Vox Humana	73
4 ft. Clarion	73
Tremolo	

CHOIR ORGAN

	PIPES
16 ft. Gamba	12
8 ft. Diapason	73
8 ft. Concert Flute	73
8 ft. Viol d'Orchestre	73
8 ft. Viol Celeste	73
8 ft. Dulciana	73
8 ft. Dulciana Celeste	73
8 ft. Quintadena	
4 ft. Flute Harmonic	73
4 ft. Violina	73
2 2/3 ft. Nazard	61
1 3/5 ft. Tierce	61
2 ft. Piccolo	61
1 1/7 ft. Septieme	61
16 ft. Fagotto	73
8 ft. Corno di Bassetto	73
8 ft. Orchestral Oboe	73
8 ft. Trumpet	73
Tremolo	

SOLO ORGAN

	PIPES
8 ft. Stentorphone	73
8 ft. Flauto Mirabilis	73
8 ft. Gamba	73
8 ft. Gamba Celeste	73
4 ft. Orchestral Flute	73
4 ft. Octave	73
Mixture (V Ranks)	305

SOLO ORGAN (Continued)

	PIPES
8 ft. French Horn	61
8 ft. English Horn	61
16 ft. Tuba	73
8 ft. Tuba	73
8 ft. Tuba Mirabilis	73
4 ft. Clarion	73
Tremolo	

PEDAL ORGAN

	PIPES
32 ft. Diapason	12
16 ft. Bourdon	32
16 ft. Diapason	32
16 ft. Contra Bass	32
16 ft. Gamba (Choir)	
16 ft. Echo Lieblich (Swell)	
16 ft. Diapason (Great)	
10 2/3 ft. Quint	12
8 ft. Gedecht (Bourdon)	12
8 ft. Octave (Open)	12
8 ft. Still Gedecht (Swell)	
8 ft. Principal	32
5 1/3 ft. Twelfth	
4 ft. Flute (Bourdon)	12
Harmonics (15, 17, 19, 21, 22)	160
32 ft. Bombarde	12
32 ft. Fagotto	12
16 ft. Trombone	32
16 ft. Tuba (Solo)	
16 ft. Fagotto (Choir)	
10 2/3 ft. Quint Trombone	12
8 ft. Trombone	24
4 ft. Clarion	12

SUMMARY OF PIPES

Great Organ	1554
Swell Organ	1681
Choir Organ	1132
Solo Organ	1157
Pedal Organ	472
Total	**5996**

MECHANICAL

Pedal Couplers, Unison and Octave
Swell, Choir, Solo to Great, 16, 8, 4
16 ft. and 4 ft. on Swell, Choir and Solo
Solo to Swell 16 ft., 8 ft., 4 ft.
Solo to Choir 16 ft., 8 ft., 4 ft.
Swell to Choir 16 ft., 8 ft., 4 ft.
Pedal to Pedal 8 ft.
Unison Releases on all manuals,
  except Great.

ADJUSTABLE AND VISIBLE COMBINATIONS

Swell — 1, 2, 3, 4, 5, 6, 7, 8
Great — 1, 2, 3, 4, 5, 6, 7
Choir — 1, 2, 3, 4, 5, 6
Solo — 1, 2, 3, 4, 5, 6
Pedal — 1, 2, 3, 4, 5, 6 7, 8
General: 1, 2, 3, 4, 5, 6, 7, 8, 9, 10
Couplers: 1, 2, 3
Double touch on Manual pistons to pick up
  pedal combinations
General Cancel, including Crescendo and
  Sforzando
Reversibles by foot and hand pistons
  Choir to Pedal
  Great to Pedal
  Swell to Pedal
  Solo to Pedal
32 ft. Stops off; 16 ft. Manual Stops off
Sforzando by pedal and piston
Swell, Choir, Solo expression pedals
Crescendo expression pedal
Adjustable connections for swell pedals
Pedal division, lower octaves
Reversibles for 32 ft. Bombarde,
  32 ft. Diapason, 32 ft. Fagotto
Adjustable Bench

Additions, Corrections, and Notes.

Bibliography.

An Account of the College of New Jersey: In which are described the Methods of Government, Modes of Instruction, Manner of Expenses of Living in the same, &c. Woodbridge, New Jersey: James Parker, 1764.

The Alumni Princetonian. "The Autobiography of Karl A. Langlotz," *Old Nassau.* New York: Wilford Seymour Conrow, [1905].

Boadway, E. A. "The Skinner and Aeolian-Skinner Opus List," *The Boston Organ Club Newsletter* v. 8, no. 9 (November, 1972), p. 3.

"Build for Princeton, N.J.," *The Diapason* v. 3, no. 3 (1 February 1912), p. 1.

Classified List of Hall Organs. West Haven, Connecticut: The Hall Organ Company, [1928?].

Coleman, Earle E. "New & Notable: *A Dialogue on Peace* (1763) and Princeton Commencements," *The Princeton University Library Chronicle* v. 46, no. 2 (Winter, 1985), pp. 231-236.

Collins, Varnum Lansing. *Princeton.* New York: Oxford University Press, 1914.

"Contracts Go To Haskell," *The Diapason* v. 10, no. 8 (1 July 1919), p. 8.

"Correspondence of the Dauphinville Courier — Our Organ," *The Princeton Standard*, Friday, 29 April 1864, p. 2.

Cuyler, Margery P., and Nathanial Burt. *The History of Trinity Church, Princeton, New Jersey: 1833-1914.* Published by the church.

The Daily Princetonian.

The Diapason.

Duffield, Rev. John T. *A Discourse on the History of the Second Presbyterian Church of Princeton, N.J.* Princeton: The Princeton Press, 1876.

"Fair for the Organ Fund," *Princeton Standard*, 10 June 1864, p. 3.

"Francis Cuyler Van Dyck," *The Diapason* v. 7, no. 4 (1 March 1916), p. 8.

Ferguson, John Allen. *Walter Holtkamp: American Organ Builder.* [Kent, Ohio]: The Kent State University Press, [1979]

"First Church Organ," *Princeton Press*, Saturday, 3 May 1902, p. 4.

Grand Concert and Organ Exhibition in the Princeton College Chapel, Tuesday Evening, Jan. 17th, 1871.

Hageman, John Frelinghuysen. *History of Princeton and its Institutions . . .* Philadelphia: J.B. Lippincott, 1879.

Hillgreen, Lane & Co., Factory Opus List, provided by Robert Hillgreen, Jr.

Hillgreen-Lane Organs; Churches, Halls, and Residences. Cleveland, Ohio: L. S. & B. Illustrating Co., [1905?].

"Improvements in Alexander Hall," *The Daily Princetonian*, Wednesday, 7 October 1896, p. 1.

"Large Crowd . . .," *The Princeton Press*, 23 March 1912, p. 2.

Link, Arthur S. *The First Presbyterian Church of Princeton: Two Centuries of History*. Princeton, New Jersey: The First Presbyterian Church, 1967.

List of More Than 5400 Möller Pipe Organs, 1880-1928. Hagerstown, Maryland: M. P. Möller, 1928.

A List of Organs Installed by Austin Organ Company, Hartford, Conn. [Hartford, Connecticut]: Published by the firm, 1919.

The Literary Diary of Ezra Stiles, D.D., LL.D., President of Yale College. Edited by Franklin Bowditch Dexter, v. 1 & 3. New York: Charles Scribner's Sons, 1901.

"Luberoff Has New Record," *The Diapason* v. 11, no. 3 (1 February 1920), p. 1.

MS, Correspondence, Hall & Labagh, New York, New York.

MS, Correspondence, Rev. Dr. John Maclean, Princeton University.

MS, *Factory Opus List,* Hillgreen-Lane, Alliance, Ohio.

MS, Financial Ledger, Princeton University.

MS, Minutes, Second Presbyterian Church, Princeton, New Jersey.

MS, Session Minutes, First Presbyterian Church, Princeton, New Jersey.

MS, Trustee Minutes, Princeton University, Princeton, New Jersey.

MS, Vestry Minutes, Trinity Church, Princeton, New Jersey.

MS, Webber Stoplist Collection.

Messiter, A. H. *A History of the Choir and Music of Trinity Church, New York From Its Organization, to the Year 1897*. New York: Edwin S. Gorham, Publisher, 1906.

The New Grove Dictionary of American Music, "James Lyon," by Richard Crawford. London: MacMillan Limited, and New York: Grove's Dictionaries of Music, Inc., 1986.

"A New Organ For Marquand Chapel," *The Alumni Princetonian*, 29 April 1897, p. 2.

"New Organ in Marquand Chapel," *Princeton Press*, Saturday, 7 August 1897, p. 2.

"New Organ for the College Chapel," *The Princeton Press*, 30 November 1860, p. 2.

"New Pipe Organ for St. Paul's," *Princeton Press*, 31 August 1917, p. 6.

Ochse, Orpha. *The History of the Organ in the United States*. Bloomington & London: Indiana University Press, [1975].

Ogasapian, John. *Organ Building in New York City: 1700-1900*. Braintree, Massachusetts: The Organ Literature Foundation, [1977].

"Opening of the Church," *Princeton Press*, 12 June 1875, p. 3.

"Organ Fund Concert," *Princeton Standard*, Friday, 18 March 1870, p. 3.

"Organ in Residence is Made by Midmer," *The Diapason* v. 7, no. 10 (1 September 1916), p. 14.

"Organ Recital," *The Alumni Princetonian*, 18 November 1897, p. 7.

"Organ Recital," *The Daily Princetonian*, Thursday, 21 April 1898, p. 1.

"Organ Recital," *Princeton Press*, 16 March 1912, p. 1.

"Organ Recital at St. Paul's," *Princeton Packet*, 12 October 1917, p. 1.

"Organ Recital at Trinity Church," *Princeton Press*, 1 March 1918, p. 6.

Osgood, Charles G. *The First Church*. Princeton: [Published by the Church], 1937.

Pierson, B. T. *Directory of the City of Newark, For 1855-56*. Newark, New Jersey: A. Stephen Holbrook, 1855.

Pilcher, William. *Samuel Davies, Apostle of Dissent in Colonial Virginia*. Knoxville [Tennessee]: The University of Tennessee Press, [1971].

The Princeton Packet.

The Princeton Press.

The Princeton Standard.

"*Residence Organ of Century Ago for Vassar Museum*," *The Diapason*, v. 23, no. 7 (1 June 1932), p. 23.

Sonneck, O. G. *Francis Hopkinson and James Lyon: Two Studies in American Music*. Washington D.C.: H. L. McQueen, 1905.

"Vacation Changes," *Princeton Press*, Saturday, 18 September 1897, p. 2.

Wertenbaker, Thomas Jefferson. *Princeton: 1746-1896*. New Jersey: Princeton University Press, 1946.

Publication of this book has been made possible by the support of the following

Subscribers.

Lester Ackerman, Jr.
Midland, Texas

Elizabeth J. Adair
Carthage, Missouri

Joseph J. Adam
Bellevue, Washington

Richard Alexander
Philadelphia, Pennsylvania

Jonathan Ambrosino
Newton, Massachusetts

American Organ Archives
Princeton, New Jersey

B. Wayne Anderson
Princeton, New Jersey

J. Theodore Anderson
Reston, Virginia

Kathy L. Anderson
Princeton, New Jersey

Norman A. André, Jr.
Valhalla, New York

Daniel L. Angerstein
Hagerstown, Maryland

John Apple
Charlotte, North Carolina

Felix Aprahamian
London, England

Lawrence Archbold
Northfield, Minnesota

Agnes Armstrong
Altamont, New York

Susan Armstrong
West Newbury, Massachusetts

Steve Arrington
No. Hollywood, California

Amory T. Atkins
Harrisville, New Hampshire

A. Thompson-Allen Co.
New Haven, Connecticut

Austin Organs, Inc.
Hartford, Connecticut

John G. Ballard
San Antonio, Texas

Charles M. Banks
Westfield, New Jersey

Nelson Barden
Newton, Massachusetts

David M. Barnett
Richmond, Virginia

J. Michael Barone
St. Paul, Minnesota

Donald C. Barnum, Jr.
New York, New York

Wilson Barry
Exeter, New Hampshire

Benjamin S. Basile
Whiting, Indiana

Mark H. Baumbach
Voorheesville, New York

Dorothea & Jack Beard
Syracuse, New York

Jerry T. Bell
Dallas, Texas

Raffi Berberian
Boston, Massachusetts

Jack Bethards
San Francisco, California

Robert W. Billings
Vincentown, New Jersey

Tony Bingham
London, England

Kevin Birch
Dedham, Massachusetts

Dr. Roberta Bitgood
Quaker Hill, Connecticut

Ted W. Blankenship, Jr.
Albany, Texas

Joseph E. Blanton
Albany, Texas

E. A. Boadway
Claremont, New Hampshire

Willis Bodine
Gainesville, Florida

Charles F. Boehm
Oceanside, California

Klaas Bolt
Haarlem, The Netherlands

Norman A. Bolton
Oakwood, Georgia

Boston Organ Club
Harrisville, New Hampshire

Boston Organ Club Library
Claremont, New Hampshire

Boston Public Library
Boston, Massachusetts

Richard Boutwell
Richmond, New Hampshire

Ruth H. Bowers
Beverly, Massachusetts

George Bozeman, Jr.
Deerfield, New Hampshire

Bill Brame
Kinston, North Carolina

James M. Bratton
Denver, Colorado

Mark Brombaugh
Rockford, Illinois

Raymond J. & Ruth Brunner
Lancaster, Pennsylvania

Fred N. Buch
Ephrata, Pennsylvania

Nelson E. Buechner
Collingswood, New Jersey

William J. Bunch
Seattle, Washington

Roger S. Burg
St. Paul, Minnesota

Larry S. Burt
Broomfield, Colorado

Alfred J. Buttler, III
New Brunswick, New Jersey

Peter T. Cameron
Lawrence, Massachusetts

Paul D. Carey
Troy, New York

Moises M. Carrasco, III
Newburyport, Massachusetts

Douglas R. Carrington
Lancashire, England

Rev. Thomas J. Carroll, S.J.
Los Angeles, California

Dr. Robert Chase
White Plains, California

Joseph & Priscilla Christopher
Greenbrae, California

Stephen T. Clark
Schenectady, New York

Richard L. Clarke
Prairie Village, Kansas

William B. Clarke, Jr.
Savannah, Georgia

Newell H. Claudy
Elkhart, Indiana

Marion L. Clemens
Davison, Michigan

William F. Clisham, Jr.
Phoenix, Maryland

James Beidler Cochran
Rochester, New York

Robert E. Coleberd
Granada Hills, California

Earle E. Coleman
Princeton, New Jersey

Henry M. Cook
Philadelphia, Pennsylvania

Chester W. Cooke
Branford, Connecticut

Giles Cooke
Williamsburg, Virginia

Matthew H. Corl
Lakeland, Florida

June W. Cortelyou
Oldsmar, Florida

David Craighead
Rochester, New York

Peter Crisafulli
Gaithersburg, Maryland

Donald D. Curry
Lincroft, New Jersey

Curtis Organ Restoration
Society of the
University of Pennsylvania
Philadelphia, Pennsylvania

William F. Czelusniak
Southampton, Massachusetts

Ted Czerkowicz
College Park, Maryland

Dartmouth College Library
Hanover, New Hampshire

Harold de La Chapelle
Cheshire, Connecticut

David P. Dahl
Tacoma, Washington

De Mixtuur
Schagen, The Netherlands

Raymond A. Di Luzio
Springfield, Massachusetts

Mary Ann Dodd
Hamilton, New York

John F. Downing
Quebec, Canada

Michael Doyle
Upland, California

Thomas Dressler
Cranbury, New Jersey

Allen G. Dreyfuss
Kew Gardens, New York

Francis E. Dugal
Florence, Massachusetts

Agnes Dumon
Grimbergen, Belgium

Charles Eames
Houston, Texas

Charles Eberline
Santa Ana, California

Michael Edgeloe
Lane Cove, Australia

Lynn Edwards
Easthampton, Massachusetts

Mr. & Mrs. William D. Edwards
Scotia, New York

E. Power Biggs Library,
Boston University
Boston, Massachusetts

G. L. Edwardson
Oakland, California

B. H. Elker
Milford, Connecticut

Francis M. Elliott,
in memory of
Martha McClosky Fishburn
Manassas, Virginia

Ronald R. Ellis
Hagerstown, Maryland

Robert A. Eversman
Hoffman Estates, Illinois

John & Kristen Farmer
Winston-Salem, North Carolina

Melissa Fearing
East Windsor, New Jersey

F. R. Feenstra
Grootegast, The Netherlands

James Fenimore, M.D.
Houston, Texas

Susan Ferré
Garland, Texas

Firestone Library,
Princeton University
Princeton, New Jersey

Thomas & Frances Finch
Canton, New York

David H. Fox
Linden Hill, New York

Arthur Frantz
Warren, Connecticut

Richard M. Frary, Jr.
Southampton, Massachusetts

D. Randall Fredrickson
Rochester, New York

Free Library of Philadelphia
Philadelphia, Pennsylvania

Free Public Library
Trenton, New Jersey

Michael & Susan Friesen
Hoffman Estates, Illinois

Dr. William S. Fuller
Princeton, New Jersey

Gary H. Geivet
Orange, California

Die Gesellschaft der Orgelfreunde
Mengen, West Germany

Dr. Tula Giannini
Princeton, New Jersey

Charles W. Gibson
Collingswood, New Jersey

In memory of
Larry Gile,
Louisville, Kentucky

Donald M. Gillett
Hagerstown, Maryland

Clifford Golden
Phoenix, Arizona

Jerzy Golos
Warsaw, Poland

Robert S. Goodwin
Dallas, Texas

Elizabeth Gorey
Bellevue, Washington

Melissa Gorey
Bellevue, Washington

Vernon Gotwals
Stonington, Maine

Carl R. Gravander, Jr.
Clearwater, Florida

Robert Gruver
Cranbury, New Jersey

Paul Gunzelmann
Columbus, Ohio

Virginia Haaland
Amenia, New York

James Hammann
Lincoln Park, Michigan

Gregory A. Hand
Mooresville, North Carolina

Dr. Roger C. Hannahs
Saratoga Springs, New York

Pierre Hardouin
Paris, France

William B. Hargett
Beaumont, Texas

Randy A. Harms
Jamesburg, New Jersey

Raymond Allen Harris, III
Chapel Hill, North Carolina

Justin Hartz
Levittown, Pennsylvania

Will O. Headlee
Syracuse, New York

Andrew Hicks
Bristol, Tennessee

Historical Society of Princeton
Princeton, New Jersey

Russell Hodges
Arkadelphia, Arkansas

Robert Hoffstetter
København, Denmark

Walter Holtkamp
Cleveland, Ohio

William L. Huber
Sag Harbor, L.I., New York

Olavi Huhtala
Scotia, New York

Dana J. Hull
Ann Arbor, Michigan

Robert W. Hunt
Mill Valley, California

Richard F. Hurley
Freehold, New Jersey

Image Graphics
Princeton, New Jersey

Harrison Jahn
Fort Atkinson, Wisconsin

Jessie Ball duPont Library
Sewanee, Tennessee

Johannes Klais, Orgelbau
Bonn, West Germany

Michael Johnston
Charlotte, North Carolina

C. de Jong
Haarlem, The Netherlands

Jan Jongepier
Leeuwarden, The Netherlands

David L. Junchen
Pasadena, California

Martin Kares
Munich, West Germany

Mary Ellen Kennedy
Quechee, Vermont

Carl George Khalil
Hightstown, New Jersey

K. Bryan Kirk
Bridgeport, Connecticut

John Kriebel
Seattle, Washington

The Rev. Michael G. Krull
Old Bridge, New Jersey

Mr. & Mrs. Stanley Landgraf
Scotia, New York

Günter Lade
Vienna, Austria

Mark Edward Laubach
Wilkes-Barre, Pennsylvania

Alan M. Laufman
Harrisville, New Hampshire

Laurie Music Library,
Rutgers University,
New Brunwswick, New Jersey

Arthur P. Lawrence
New York, New York

James R. Lawrence
Bronx, New York

Fred B. Le Compt
Lawrenceville, New Jersey

Dr. Robin A. Leaver
Princeton, New Jersey

Laurence Leonard
Laconia, New Hampshire

Jim Lewis
Pasadena, California

Library of Congress
Washington, D.C.

Joan & Curtis Lippincott
Skillman, New Jersey

Bruce K. Lockhart
Brooklyn, New York

B. Lotti
Bologna, Italy

Betty Loveland
Bridgeton, New Jersey

Karl Loveland
Rochester, New York

Kurt Lueders
Levallois Perret, France

Thilo Lützkendorf
Halle, East Germany

Oluf Chris Lund
Solvang, California

Linwood D. Lunde
Richmond, Virginia

Thomas McBeth
Princeton, New Jersey

David McCain
Orlando, Florida

In loving memory of
Randall Jay McCarty
from David C. Calhoun
Seattle, Washington

Robert P. McDermitt
Princeton, New Jersey

Lloyd L. McGaughy
Galt, California

Charles W. McManis
Walnut Creek, California

David Y. McManis
Lanham, Maryland

Forrest Mack
Waltham, Massachusetts

John Maidment
Victoria, Australia

Paul N. Maine
Buffalo, New York

Thomas Matthews
Atlanta, Georgia

Lorenz Maycher
Muskogee, Oklahoma

Shirley Mazzga
Hawley, Pennsylvania

R. W. Melbye, M.D.
South Pasadena, California

Jesse B. Mercer
Elizabeth City, North Carolina

Messrs. Czelusniak et Dugal, Inc.
Northampton, Massachusetts

Michael Michaud
Lynn, Massachusetts

Earl L. Miller
Andover, Massachusetts

Robert G. Miller
New Britain, Pennsylvania

John H. Mitchell
Orlando, Florida

Walter J. Mitchell
Fall River, Massachusetts

Theodore A. Montgomery, M.D.
Piedmont, California

Grant R. Moss
Northampton, Massachusetts

Thomas Murray
Guilford, Connecticut

Music Library,
University of California
Los Angeles, California

Nassau Presbyterian Church
(Merger of Old First Church
and Second Presbyterian Church)
Princeton, New Jersey

H. Wells Near
Cleveland Heights, Ohio

A. Scott Nelson
Sacramento, California

George Nelson
Seattle, Washington

Nelson Barden Associates, Inc.
Newton, Massachusetts

Rev. Mark R. Nemmers
Dubuque, Iowa

New Jersey Historical Society
New Brunswick, New Jersey

New York Public Library
New York, New York

Noack Organ Co., Inc.
Georgetown, Massachusetts

Keith E. Norrington
New Albany, Indiana

Oberlin College Library
Oberlin, Ohio

Orpha Ochse
Whittier, California

Dr. John Ogasapian
Pepperell, Massachusetts

Spencer J. Olney
Largo, Florida

Catherine O'Neill
Trenton, New Jersey

Organ Clearing House
Harrisville, New Hampshire

Organ Literature Foundation
Braintree, Massachusetts

Organ Historical Society, Inc.
Richmond, Virginia

Freeman R. Orr, Jr.
Greenville, South Carolina

William Osborne
Granville, Ohio

Richard Ouellette
West Newbury, Massachusetts

Barbara Owen
Newburyport, Massachusetts

Jan Pak
Neshanic Station, New Jersey

John A. Panning
Lake City, Iowa

Robert E. Parr
South Miami, Florida

Carrie Peapples
Raymond, New Hampshire

Harold L. Penny
East Amherst, New York

Petty-Madden Organbuilders, Inc.
Hopewell, New Jersey

Mr. & Mrs. Kenneth Phillips
Scotia, New York

Gerald L. Piercey
Kensington, Maryland

Mrs. Arthur F. Pinel
Hingham, Massachusetts

Courtney Pinel
Ballston Spa, New York

Edgar L. Pinel, Jr.
Scotia, New York

Mr. & Mrs. Edgar L. Pinel, Sr.
Quincy, Massachusetts

James S. Pinel
North Providence, Rhode Island

John & Irene Pinel
Ballston Spa, New York

Joseph & Alice Pinel
Quincy, Massachusetts

Leatrice O. Pinel
Scotia, New York

Mandy Pinel
Ballston Spa, New York

Samantha Pinel
Ballston Spa, New York

Wilfried Praet
Zwijndrecht, Belgium

Princeton Public Library
Princeton, New Jersey

Princeton University Archives
Princeton, New Jersey

Princeton University Chapel,
Music Department
Princeton, New Jersey

Princeton University Store
Princeton, New Jersey

Michele E. Prokopchack
Colesville, Maryland

Nellie Verloop Prout
Schagen, The Netherlands

Michael Quimby
Warrensburg, Missouri

Philip Quirk
Liverpool, England

Nathan A. Randall
Princeton, New Jersey

John L. Randolph
Brooklyn, New York

Anita Randolfi
New York, New York

Stephen Rapp
Rye, New York

Jaap Remmelzwaal
Amersfoort, The Netherlands

Martin Renshaw
Kent, England

Joyce Painter Rice
Brookline, Massachusetts

Eugene Roan
Princeton, New Jersey

Albert F. Robinson
Peekskill, New York

Rosales Organ Builders, Inc.
Los Angeles, California

Paul Rosendall
San Francisco, California

Jack Russ
Bridgeton, New Jersey

Paul Sahlin
Concord, California

Saint Dunstan Art Organ Works
Houston, Texas

Randall V. Sandt
Belvidere, New Jersey

Allen R. Savage
Skippack, Pennsylvania

Rev. Alfred von Schendel
Loretto, Pennsylvania

Dr. Charles Schisler
Atlanta, Georgia

Arthur E. Schlueter, Jr.
Lithonia, Georgia

Schoenstein & Co., Organbuilders
San Francisco, California

Gordon A. Schultz
Roseville, Minnesota

Jeffrey A. Scofield
Chattanooga, Tennessee

Joseph M. Scutti
Newfield, New Jersey

David & Permelia Sears
Dunstable, Massachusetts

John P. Seiz
Highland Heights, Ohio

Horace W. Sellers
East Woodstock, Connecticut

Charlie L. Shue
Dallas, Texas

Michael Simpson
Richmond, Virginia

Richard A. Smid
Boyton Beach, Florida

Emmet G. Smith
Fort Worth, Texas

J. Jay Smith
Trenton, New Jersey

Neal J. Smith
Cherry Hill, New Jersey

Rollin Smith
Brooklyn, New York

Timothy Edward Smith
Milford, Connecticut

Smithsonian Institution Libraries
Washington, D.C.

David Synder
Buffalo, New York

Dr. & Mrs. Loren Southern
Skillman, New Jersey

H. Spek
Dordrecht, The Netherlands

Dr. John Speller
Reading, Pennsylvania

Michael Stairs
Rosemont, Pennsylvania

Kent Stalker
Lubbock, Texas

Kenneth Starr
Boston, Massachusetts

Ken and Carol Stein
Fort Wayne, Indiana

Julie Stephens
Western Springs, Illinois

Bruce Stevens
Richmond, Virginia

Elizabeth Stodola
Little Rock, Arkansas

John A. Stokes
Princeton, New Jersey

Raymond Sultra
Toulouse, France

David R. Sultzbach
Lancaster, Pennsylvania

Norman Sutphin
Houston, Texas

Talbott Library,
Westminster Choir College
Princeton, New Jersey

Susan Tattershall
Staatsburg, New York

Carol Teti
Indiana, Pennsylvania

Thomas J. Watson Library,
Metropolitan Museum of Art
New York, New York

Thomas-Pierce, Ltd /
Austin Organs, Inc.
Palm Beach, Florida

Chuck Thompson
North Kingstown, Rhode Island

Lynn Thompson
Louisville, Kentucky

David Tiedman
Milford, Massachusetts

V. H. M. Timmer
Leek, The Netherlands

Jack Townsend
Fullerton, California

Donald R. Traser
Richmond, Virginia

Fern R. Traugot
New Orleans, Louisiana

Larry Trupiano
Brooklyn, New York

Roger P. Turney
Princeton, New Jersey

Charles J. Updegraph
South Orange, New Jersey

Ralph B. Valentine
Willingford, Connecticut

Edna Van Duzee Walter
Round Lake, New York

Gerard Verloop
Schagen, The Netherlands

Charles Vermeulen
Bruges, Belgium

Arie M. Voskuil
Elkhart, Indiana

Robert M. Voves
Westchester, Illinois

Randall E. Wagner
Erie, Pennsylvania

Robert E. Waller
Hoosick Falls, New York

Eric Walling
Walnut Creek, California

James L. Wallman
Gaithersburg, Maryland

Peter Walker
Princeton, New Jersey

John Powell Walsh
St. Louis, Missouri

Martin R. Walsh
Watertown, Massachusetts

Norman Walter
Round Lake, New York

Dr. Richard Webb
Lawrenceville, New Jersey

Malcolm Wechsler
Baltimore, Maryland

Bob Webber
Concord, California

J. Ernest Wells, D.C., J.D.
Nicholasville, Kentucky

Harold A. Wentz
Edwardsville, Illinois

Werner Josten Library,
Smith College
Northampton, Massachusetts

Westfield Center for
Early Keyboard Studies
Easthampton, Massachusetts

Westminster Music and Books
Princeton, New Jersey

George F. Wharton, III
Frenchtown, New Jersey

Warren R. White
Piedmont, California

Mrs. R. V. C. Whitehead, Jr.
Princeton, New Jersey

Robert Bruce Whitting
Schwenksville, Pennsylvania

Nancy Wicklund
Sergeantsville, New Jersey

Martin Wiegand
Millville, New Jersey

The Rev. Bruce McK. Williams
Albuquerque, New Mexico

Mark Williams
Trenton, New Jersey

J. Clark Wilson
E. Liverpool, Ohio

James & Carolyn Wilson
Easton, Connecticut

Ellen Pinel Wittington
Bellevue, Washington

Edward P. Wood
Kansas City, Missouri

Douglas M. Woodard
Boulder, Colorado

H. C. J. Wullink
Zwolle, The Netherlands

Yale University Music Library
New Haven, Connecticut

Martin D. Ybarra
San Antonio, Texas

The Rev. Carol H. Youse
Baltimore, Maryland

Dean Theodore Ziolkowski
Princeton, New Jersey

Yetta Ziolkowski
Princeton, New Jersey

Mark Zwilling
El Paso, Texas

Index.

Old Organs of Princeton was typeset in Bembo by
Image Graphics, Princeton, New Jersey.
Printing and binding were done by
BookCrafters

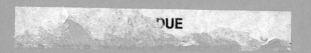
DUE